Swing and Day Trading

TABLE OF CONTENTS

3

GETTING STARTED WITH DAY TRADING
DAY TRADING STRATEGIES

CHAPTER SEVEN: MAXIMIZING POTENTIAL RETURN WITH SHORT SELLING AND LEVERAGE

THE SWITCH-UP OF SHORT SELLING

RISK AND REWARD ASSESSMENT FROM SHORT SELLING AND LEVERAGE

CONCLUSION - STRATEGIES OF 2020 THAT WORKS

ABOUT THIS BOOK

In Swing And Day Trading 2020, I introduce you to the strategies and techniques of the swing and day trader for beginners and then advanced traders. Moreover, I discussed the topics given short shrift in some swing trading textbooks — topics that broadly define your swing trading success. For instance, whereas many textbooks focus on technical indicators and chart patterns used in shorting or buying stocks, this book goes one step beyond to cover how to save and optimize the time, technical and fundamental analysis, and strategy planning.

Although these subjects are less glamorous than looking at charts, they're more important — because even exceedingly experienced chart readers will fail if they devise a flawed system, take unnecessary risks, and don't learn from their mistakes. This book has been written to help traders manage risks and avoid unnecessary mistakes.

Here are some of the areas covered in this book:

• Technical Analysis: Determining Your Entry and Exit Points

• Fundamental Analysis: Digging Deeper into the Market

- Developing and Implementing Your Trading Plan

- Strengthening Your Defense: Managing Risk

- Fine-Tuning Your Entries and Exits

- Maximizing Potential Return with Short Selling and Leverage

- And more…

INTRODUCTION

Making a lot of money is the obvious goal of most people who decide to enter the world of trading. Your success as a swing or day trader depends on your ability to use the tools, collect the information you need, and interpret what you have. You must develop the discipline to apply all you know about trading in the development of a winning trading strategy.

Knowing how to avoid getting caught up in the emotional aspects of trading - the ups and downs of a loss - is the key to developing a lucrative trading style. Trading is an activity and should be approached with the same logic that you would apply in your approach to any other management decision. Setting goals, researching your options, planning and implementing your strategies, and evaluating your success are as important to trading as any other business.

In this book, we help you overcome these obstacles while introducing beginner strategies and advanced strategies, as well as methods to save time and optimize trading time. In this book, we present an overview of trading and an introduction to the tools you need, the research skills you should use, and the basics of turning all this information into a successful trading strategy.

CHAPTER ONE - THE BASICS OF SWING TRADING

You can make a living in this world in different ways. The most common way is to master certain skills - like medicine in the case of doctors, or computer science in the case of information technology specialists - and to trade your time for money. The more your experience, the higher your salary. The advantage of mastering a skill is clear: you are relatively safe relative to income. Of course, there is no guarantee. Their capacity can be exceeded (I do not believe that many horse car manufacturers operate today) or their work can be shipped overseas. You also have maximum earning potential given the maximum number of hours you can work without exhausting yourself.

But there is another way to make a living. Swing Trading offers you the advantage of earning an income based not on the number of hours you invest, but on the quality of your business. The more you negotiate, the greater your potential. Swing trading takes utilizes short-term price movements and seeks a good return on investment over a short period.

Swing trading is a good option for a minority of the population. This involves enormous amounts of responsibility. You need to be confident and not be reckless or gambling. You may not generate any income (or worse) if you are not disciplined.

This book is designed to help those of you interested in swing trading. To understand swing trading, you must understand what is and what is not.

What is Swing Trading?

Swing trading is described as the art and science of taking advantage of short-term bond price movements, ranging from a few days to a few weeks, one or two months at most. Swing traders can be institutions or individuals, such as hedge funds. They are rarely 100% invested in the market at any time. Instead, they expect low-risk opportunities and try to increase the lion's share of a significant upward or downward movement. When the market is generally on the rise, they buy a lot more often than they are short. When the market is generally weak, they are shorter than they buy. And if the market does not do so much, they stand patiently aside.

Swing trading is different from buy-and-hold or day trading. These types of investors approach markets differently, trade at different frequencies, and pay close attention to different data sources. You must understand that these differences are not focused on issues that only affect long-term investors.

How does Swing Trading differ from Day Trading?

The day trader is the opposite of the buy-and-hold investor in the trading continuum. Day traders do not occupy any position overnight. This would eventually expose them to the risk of a spread between the price of a security, which could erase a large part of their account. Instead, they monitor minute-by-minute price movements and inbound and outbound movements every hour.

Day traders have the advantage of having price movements of securities that can be quite volatile. This requires a hard time on their part. Short-term price movements can be caused by a big seller or buyer in the market and not by the fundamentals of a company. Thus day traders are more concerned with investor psychology than with fundamentals. They follow the noise of the market - they wonder if the noise gets louder and louder.

But all is not just cake and tea for day traders. They negotiate so often that they accumulate high commission rates, which makes it much harder to beat the market in general. A profit of $ 5,000 generated by hundreds of transactions can give a day trader a considerably reduced amount after the withdrawal of commissions and taxes. This does not include the additional costs that the professional of the day has to support to support its activities.

Swing traders also incur high fees (compared to the buy-and-hold investor), but nothing as severe as the day trader. Since price movements vary from a few days to several weeks, the fundamentals of a company can extend on a larger scale than for the day trader (day-to-day movements are due less to fundamentals and more to the demand of shares and short-term supply). Also, the swing trader can generate greater potential profits in individual transactions because the holding period is longer than that of the market operator.

What is Swing Trading for you?

Determine your time commitment

Starting to negotiate on the swing requires some thought. Before you rush to buy the PC or set up this brokerage account, you need to think about the type of swing professional you want to be. (Yes, swing marketers come in different shapes and sizes.)

Your first step is to determine how much time you can commit to changing things. You can be a full-time trader for a company, in which case you should consider yourself a lifelong trader. Or you may be making this part-time income with the hope (and intention) of becoming a full-time trader.

Many swing traders own full-time jobs and have little time to trade. They, therefore, negotiate primarily to improve the return on their investment accounts. Or maybe they are already retired and are they trying to increase their assets over time? These swing traders monitor the market during the day but rely on orders placed outside trading hours to enter or exit their positions. And if they manage deferred tax accounts, such as an individual withdrawal account, they can ignore the tax issue.

The fact is that you can change jobs, whether you have a full-time job or not, but you have to make adjustments depending on whether you can look at the market all day long. And besides, watching the market all day does not necessarily improve your returns. It can diminish them if it forces you to exaggerate excessively or to react to the oscillations of the market.

Swing Trading as your main source of income

If you want to trade as your primary means of generating income, prepare to spend several months or even years gaining experience before you can quit your job and bargain at home full time. Full-time traders spend several hours a day trading. They look for possible offers before, during, and after market hours. And they handle the pressure well.

Many traders believe that they can not cope with the stress of full-time trading. After all, if swing trading is your primary source of income, you have to face many pressures to generate consistent profits. And you might be more tempted to bet if you have a lot of losses. What many traders do not realize is that the right answer to a lot of losses is not more trading but less trading. Go back and evaluate the situation.

Swing trading for a living is not difficult in the sense that it is necessary to have an incredible level of IQ or insane work ethic. On the contrary, it requires an incredible amount of self-control, discipline, and calm. A swing tradesperson who trades for income should always be emotionless. When things are not going well, he does not try to recover, but he turns to another opportunity.

So do not quit your job simply because you are generating impressive profits for a few months. The name of this game is always to have enough capital to go back and replay. If you are thinking of living with $ 5,000 a month, for example, you can not generate that kind of profit with $ 30,000 of capital. This would require a monthly gain of 16.67%! Some of the best traders of all time in the world have achieved returns of 20 to 25% per year for 20 or 30 years.

Swing trading to supplement income or improve return on investment

This category probably applies to the lion's share of swing traders. Swing trading with an eye on improving returns on your portfolio or earning extra income is less stressful than doing swing trade for a living. If you perform a blunder, you still have something to do, and you can change jobs while keeping a full-time job.

Part-time swing traders usually carry out their analysis when they return home after work and set up transactions the next day. Even if they can not watch the market all the time, they can file a stop order to protect their capital.

If you want to change jobs full time, you must first go through this step. Over time, you can determine the performance of your work. And if you decide to opt for other recommendations in this book (such as keeping a translation journal, which I'll cover in later in this book), you'll learn from your mistakes and improve your techniques.

PURSUE THE STRATEGIC PLAN OF THE SWING TRADER

Plan your business and negotiate your plan.

Be prepared to plan to fail f you fail to plan.

Many pictures highlight the importance of a bargaining plan. A trading plan means the business plan of your trading business. Without this plan, you risk falling into the trap of inventing things as you go. Your negotiation will be erratic.

You will not improve because you will not have records of your previous transaction. You may think that your business plan is in your head, but if you have not written it, it does not exist.

Throughout this book, I will cover in detail all the important parts of the swing trading strategy. In the following sections, I visualize the critical parts of the strategy, reducing them to a single small package.

The "what": determines the obligations that you will exchange

Your trading plan should identify the traded securities. As a swing trader, one of the benefits you have is that you can select from a variety of titles:

Public Actions (Shares): This category is perhaps what you know best. Common shares, US deposit certificates, and exchange-traded funds are included in this section. Swing traders trade stocks exclusively because of the variety, ease, and familiarity with the trading of securities transactions. Most shares listed in the US are traded daily, but shares in foreign markets can rarely be traded (perhaps once a week).

To make your inputs and outputs as simple as possible, you only need to focus on actions that correspond to a specified volume level. Trying to sell 2,000 shares of a stock that trades 6,000 shares a day can be extremely expensive. I recommend you use stocks because of the abundance of information about companies in the domestic and even international market.

One of the strengths of equities is the efficiency with which they are traded, in part because they provide exposure to other asset classes. For instance, you can gain exposure to gold commodities by trading a fund traded with underlying assets in gold. I keep things on my own because it's my area of expertise, and I would also recommend them as a result of this exposure to other asset classes and the diversity of positions you can choose. But you may also want to trade other asset classes - it's your link.

American Depository Receipts (ADR): ADRs have become increasingly important in today's globalized world. In simple terms, an ADR allows US investors to buy shares of foreign companies. ADRs are denominated in US dollars and pay dividends in US dollars. Exchanging ADR is much more profitable than creating accounts in several foreign countries, converting your dollars into foreign currency, etc. And as the economic growth of emerging countries exceeds that of developed countries, ADRs can offer big profit opportunities. ADRs of companies based in emerging markets (such as Brazil or China) sometimes have a large leverage effect on a particular commodity, allowing them to take advantage of high commodity prices.

Exchange Traded Funds (ETFs): ETFs are global investments. Most current ETFs reflect the movement of an index (for example SPY, a popular ETF which tracks the S & P 500 Index) or the sub-sector of an index. If you want to take advantage of future technology, you will be better able to negotiate a technology ETF than to choose a particular technology company that may or may not be in the general tech sector. Indeed, if you are traveling, you will benefit from a diversified technology ETF. However, only one security technology can resist the trend. ETFs also offer the opportunity to profit from international indices and commodities.

Closed Funding: These funds are essentially mutual funds traded on a secondary stock exchange. Traditional and open-end mutual funds are valued based on their net asset value - or the amount remaining after subtracting the fund's liabilities from their assets. Closed funds are different. Their price is set according to the supply and demand for shares of this fund. Sometimes a closed fund will be exchanged for more than its net asset value; at other times, it will be negotiated for less. Closed funds can be an effective way to take advantage of international markets.

Fixed Income Markets: These markets include bonds issued by governments at the federal, state, and local levels, as well as those issued by corporations. The value of fixed income securities depends on interest rates, inflation, issuer solvency, and other factors. Because the fixed income market generally has lower volatility than equities and other asset classes, many swing traders often avoid trading it.

Futures Contracts: Standard contracts for the purchase or sale of an underlying asset on a given date in the future at a more specified price are referred to as futures contracts. Futures contracts are traded in commodities and financial instruments, such as equity indices. Technically, the buyer and the seller do not exchange money before the expiry of the contract. However, futures markets require traders to have a margin of 5% to 15% of the value of the contract. This means that traders can use extreme leverage, if they wish, with only a small portion of the value of the contract.

I strongly recommend that you avoid using such extreme leverage because of the risk of losing most, if not all, of your assets as a result of an unexpected change in security. Newcomers, in particular, should avoid using leverage. Even experienced swing professionals can become careless or arrogant before the market educates them.

Commodities: This type of security is perhaps the largest asset class that attracts attention today beyond equities. With the explosion of all prices, from gold to crude, commodities are attracting more money from swing traders. Commodities - including energy products, agricultural products, and precious metals - are traded on the futures markets.

You can take advantage of fluctuations in commodity prices through exchange-traded or exchange-traded funds. For example, swing traders who want to take advantage of gold price movements can exchange StreetTRACKS Gold shares, which track the gold price. But commercial products carry risks and problems that differ from commercial stocks. (For more information on how to trade commodities, see Amine Bouchentouf, Commodities for Dummies, published by Wiley.)

The Forex Market: Often called the forex or forex market, the foreign exchange market is the largest and the most prominent financial market in the globe. Considering the information from the Bank of International Settlements, the average daily turnover of foreign exchange markets is $ 3.21 billion. As a future market, exchange on the foreign exchange market allows for extreme leverage.

Not all brokers offer currency trading, so make sure your broker has the capacity. Unlike equities, currency market transactions are concentrated in a few currencies: the US dollar, the Japanese yen, the euro, the Swiss franc, and the pound sterling. If you plan to use fundamental analysis to supplement your technical analysis as a swing trader (see the definitions of the two terms in the "Establishing Your Analytics" section later in this chapter), get ready for learn about the various factors that affect the value of foreign currencies: inflation, political stability, public deficits and economic growth - just to name a few.

Options: Contracts that give the buyer the opportunity, but not the obligation, to buy an underlying asset at a specified price until the maturity date is called options. Options are very risky and ineffective trading vehicles because of their lack of liquidity.

The "where": decide where you are going to exchange

The place where you trade depends a lot on what you are trading. Equities, commodities, currencies, and bonds are traded in different markets.

The American Stock Exchange (AMEX), the New York Stock Exchange (NYSE), and the NASDAQ list US and foreign equities (they also list other investment vehicles, like exchange-traded funds, which enable you to generate profit from movements in prices of commodities and other asset classes). NASDAQ is distinguished from the NYSE and AMEX by its electronic integrity that enables efficient transactions and order routing.

Not all stocks are traded on these markets. Recently, electronic communications networks (ECNs) have emerged as an effective way to combine buy and sell orders. ECNs connect individual traders with leading brokers. Sometimes you can see a better price by sending orders to an ECN instead of a broker. The easiest way to access ECNs is to subscribe to a broker providing direct access to trading.

But swing traders can purchase and sell other stocks in other markets. For instance, if you want to trade a real product, the Chicago Board of Trade (CBOT) lists several products: ethanol, gold, silver, corn, wheat, oats, rice, and soy. nThe New York Mercantile Exchange (NYMEX) also lists popular products such as crude oil, coal, natural gas, and gold. But you should consider the additional risk factors if you venture out of commercial stocks. For example, products require different margins for stocks. Failure to properly use a risk management system can result in the loss of all your capital in one company. Commodities also trade with fundamentals that are different from those of companies or fixed income securities.

If you wish to trade commodities, currencies, or other investment instruments, you must negotiate with companies authorized to trade in these markets.

The "when" and the "how": choose your style and trading strategy

If you enter orders during or after business hours, this will affect your inbound and outbound policies.

Swing traders enter part-time orders when markets are closed, they trust the limit and prevent losses from executing their strategy.

Full-time traders, meanwhile, can manage their inflows and outflows during the day and incorporate an intraday price action into their trading timing.

They also find more business opportunities because they have more time to devote to swing trading.

The way you trade refers to your different trading strategies, which I describe in this section.

Establish your analysis techniques

Swing operators rely on two main analytical techniques: technical analysis and fundamental analysis. In technical terms, the technical analysis includes the analysis of graphical models and the application of mathematical formulas to security prices and volumes. The fundamental analysis covers earnings, sales, and other fundamentals of a company or security.

In my experience, most swing traders rely to a large extent on technical analysis. However, I explain the two analytical techniques described in this book because I firmly believe that understanding and using both improves the chances of success.

Both analysis techniques have their advantages:

Technical analysis can be applied quickly and easily to any market or security. For instance, a trained swing trader can make use of technical analysis to quickly decide whether to buy or sell a bond using graphical technical indicator standards. On the other hand, a swing trader who relies on fundamental analysis needs more time to know more about a company, its business, and its profits before drawing its conclusion. Whether you trade commodities, currencies, stocks, or bonds, you can apply technical analysis consistently to these markets. In other words, if you know your way around the interpretation of a graph, the type of security represented is largely irrelevant. In my opinion, ease of application is the main benefit of technical analysis on fundamental analysis.

Fundamental analysis can answer questions that go beyond technical analysis, such as, "Why is this security price evolving?" within 100 meters. Rallies and falls based on fundamentals are more profitable than rallies and fall that results from market noise (such as a mutual fund wound up or buying a position). In the long run, security movements are dictated by the underlying fundamentals of securities. Crude oil prices rise when demand is more than supply or when supply becomes scarce - no, as the technical analysis shows, which is superficial because the map has evolved optimistically. (Of course, crude oil - or any other title - can go up or down for non-fundamental reasons.) But such events and falls are often ephemeral and less powerful than price movements based on fundamentals.

Some swing traders avoid learning more about the fundamentals of society. In general, fundamental analysis is considered lengthy, laborious, and not always correct. But you can improve your swing by reaching the essence of a company's fundamentals, even if it requires extensive reading, research, and modeling.

How much should you worry about the fundamentals of business? The general rule is that the wider your investment horizon, the more fundamental the analysis becomes. The lower your horizon, the less fundamental analysis in securities trading is important. Indeed, short-term movements depend on momentum, noise, and other factors. In the long run, however, fundamentals are always winning.

But just because you understand how to apply the fundamentals is not because you are going to make money. Markets do not arise simply because they are undervalued or simply because they are overvalued. Markets may remain undervalued or overvalued for long periods. That's why I do not recommend to swing with just the basics. A fundamental analysis indicates where the wind is blowing, so you're ready, but a technical analysis provides important temporal elements.

Choose the candidates to buy

You can find promising titles in two main ways: the top-down approach and the bottom-up approach. Both are described in detail later in this book, but here is a summary:

Top-Down Approach: swing traders who prefer the top-down approach identify opportunities that begin at the market level, deepen at the industry level, and then analyze individual companies. If you fall into this category, your entry strategy should start with a review of global markets, then go to the major market sectors and then to industries in the strongest or weakest sectors. At this point, you sort the industry headings according to technical or fundamental measures. You then select the titles that fit your entry strategy.

Bottom-Up Approach: Swing traders who use the bottom-up approach are bottom-up individuals who are looking for strong stocks, then filter out promising ones based on their industry groups or sectors. If you fall into this category, your approach starts with a screen (a screen is a quantitative filter), sometimes depending on whether the stocks of growth or value are favorable at a given moment. If so, then you compare the relative strength of growth and the value ratios (and possibly also the market capitalization of the market). Once you have identified the highest ranking on the screen, you determine the securities that meet the entry rules, and you only trade in securities that belong to advanced or backward industry groups, depending on whether you prefer to buy or sell short.

Plan Your Exit

Most swing traders focus almost entirely on their entry strategy, but it's the exit strategy that determines when you make a profit, suffer losses, and when you come out of a winding position to better use your capital. It is therefore important to plan your entry, but you have to spend as much time (if not more) getting out of it.

Your exit strategy is likely to be technique driven and triple:

Determine when you are leaving for a profit. Do not take advantage of intuition; trust a trigger or a catalyst. For example, some exit strategies for profit stipulate that the time of reconciliation occurs when prices reach the implicit target in a chart or when stocks approach a moving average.

Determine when you are leaving for a loss. Your loss exit strategy should be based on exceeding the support level, a resistance level (in the case of a short circuit) or a moving average (for example, the nine-day moving average). (Support levels are priced zones where bonds stop falling, and resistance levels are price zones where prices stop rising.) This limits

31

losses to a known quantity (to fall or fall in the price of should be approached by the appropriate sizing of position and other risk management techniques).

Determine when to stop if a business does not generate profits or losses. In other words, it winds on the side and causes a dead weight. Some swing operators quickly leave a position if they do not. I prefer to give myself a few days to prove myself one way or another. Therefore, I recommend leaving a position after ten days if it does not reach the stop loss level or does not trigger a gain signal.

You must define your exit strategy by ensuring that your trading plans negotiate profits, losses, and redistribution of capital.

Establish when you will net long or short

Sometimes swing traders open bonds to take advantage of falling prices. If you choose to incorporate the short circuit into your trading strategy, you must determine when you will be net long or net short.

Long Net means that most of the assets you have invested in are on the long side of the market. Net short means that most of the assets you have invested in are on the short side of the market. And if your long and short assets are the same, you are neutral in the market.

Generally, the decision to be a long or short liquid is determined by the condition of the main market index. When the S & P 500, for example, is in a bull market, most swing traders are liquid. When the S & P 500 is down, most swing traders are liquid. And when the market is within a trading range, swing traders can be neutral in the market.

Prepare your risk management plan

The most important way to manage your risk is the most important part of your trading plan. Risk management, which I will discuss in detail later in this book, explains how you manage risk at the individual security level and the portfolio level as a whole. A business plan with a weak entry strategy and a weak exit strategy may still generate profit if the risk management strategy limits losses and makes profits.

To effectively manage your risks, you need to consider the following aspects of your trading plan:

What is your level of risk in an individual position: your trading plan should indicate the amount you plan to allocate to a single position.

What is the risk level of your overall portfolio? You determine the risk percentage of your total portfolio in a given position.

How to achieve an appropriate diversification: Diversification means more than adding multiple titles. You need exposure to different asset classes, industries, and market capitalizations.

How you combine long and short positions: The combination of long and short positions allows your portfolio to profit from high and low markets.

How do you implement the 7% rule: the risk that you run in a single position is different from your total risk for your portfolio. The 7% rule limits your overall risk by 7%.

How you determine your exit points: Your products should be guided by support and resistance bands, technical indicators, and profit targets.

What triggers an exit: An exit may occur as a result of a loss, a profit, or a significant lack of action on the market.

How do you manage your emotions? Whatever the effectiveness of a risk management system, it should ultimately be adopted by a human being. This last point is, therefore, crucial because human beings are affected by emotions, experiences, and hopes. This may cause the distributor to abandon the rigid rules it has created and may have followed for years.

I have found that emotion management is the most difficult aspect of swing trading. The more you can negotiate, the more your emotions are likely to convince you to cut costs and abandon the rules that have brought you where you are. But emotions can be managed. You can limit their impact, for example, by implementing stop loss orders that exclude you from security without any intervention on your part.

Previous markers are summarized in two share categories: sizing positions and limiting portfolio losses. So what's the difference between the two? Alexander Elder, a trade specialist, has already made the distinction between individual and portfolio-level losses thanks to an analogy between sharks and fish. Specifically, he said that the sizing of positions aims to reduce the risk that your portfolio will suffer a loss of "shark bite" due to a single position. That's one big loss that eliminates the value of your account.

On the other hand, the risk management of the portfolio is carried out in such a way as to prevent several minor losses from killing him - or, as he has described, death by piranha bites. A single little piranha may not be able to kill a bigger mammal, but dozens of piranhas working together can be deadly.

Similarly, a small loss does not represent a risk of death for a portfolio. The risk is that many small losses can regroup and cause significant losses. That's why you need to limit losses at the level of an individual stock (and avoid shark bites) while limiting losses in the wallet (to avoid death by piranha bites).

Build your Swing Trading Prowess

Staying at the top of your game implies you can never stop learning or improving. Unfortunately, you can not simply become an extraordinary turnaround operator and implement your business with just one problem. Heck, a martial arts master does not stop after winning his black belt - why a swing shopkeeper?

The following actions will help you stay strong throughout your trading career:

Accept losses when they occur. Markets even humiliate the most skilled traders if they let their ego hinder their trade. Some traders continue to lose positions hoping to break even, a policy that destroys a long-term account. A losing position can lose not only more money but also mobilize capital that could be invested in more promising trading opportunities.

Be a student of the markets. Successful swing traders never stop absorbing information. Markets are constantly changing, with the appearance of new investment vehicles and the introduction of new laws. A swing trader must maintain intellectual curiosity. Reading books is a way to stay informed. They are interested in understanding their positions and reading the arguments for and against them.

Try not to be affected by the opinions of others, whether you are an average Joe or Wall Street analyst. Do not forget that Wall Street is a community, and analysts send their opinion reports to hundreds or even thousands of traders and portfolio managers. Reading these reports can lead you to think about how the analyst - and hundreds of others. A good performance is not about copying what everyone is doing.

Do not go to bulletin boards. Bulletin Boards often promote a group mindset that a position must behave in a certain way. You do not want to collect knowledge from anyone on the Internet. Instead, stick to reliable sources and give your opinion on some issues.

CHAPTER TWO: DETERMINING YOUR ENTRY AND EXIT POINTS: TECHNICAL ANALYSIS

It is very difficult to try to make money on a commercial scale market. You not only have the almost impossible task of locating the beginning of such a period (which means, in fact,

end of a long bull market), you must also find the beginning and end of the big fluctuations that will form the trading range.

A long-term bull market, like the one we have had since 1982, spoils investors. When prices fall, investors are conditioned to the idea that if they wait, prices will go up and down again. They become neglected because investing becomes very easy - just put your money in and watch how almost everything goes higher. It's the best of all worlds. An old and wise saying of market folklore warns: "Never confuse the brains with a bull market."

When a long bull market ends and a new period begins, the importance of precise and disciplined negotiations becomes apparent again. Stocks no longer show the characteristic of a long-term upward trend. Many actions diminish and never come back. A significant number of declines has been so severe that it eliminates all gains from the previous bull market. In times like these, you should have bigger trading disciplines and rigid guidelines that will move you away quickly when your ideas are wrong.

Consider the figure below. The points at the bottom of the solid line represent my projection of the future stock price trend. To invest in a period like this, it is necessary to bring all the reliable tools to support the effort. Elliott's Wave Model is the basic model for predicting the broad outlines of what to expect from prices. However, the trader should always keep each forecast fluid; you must never write in concrete. Elliott's wave model, with the innumerable and complex variations that the theory allows, is inherently incomplete; you must incorporate other information to help limit the number of possible Elliott wave patterns. Technical analysis is an important tool in this effort.

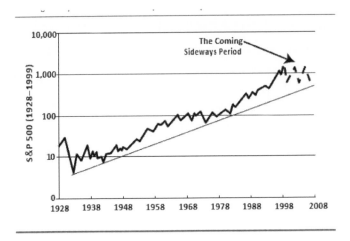

CLARIFICATION OF TIME IN TECHNICAL ANALYSIS

Returning to the stock market model presented earlier, the model argues that stock prices are equal to fair value stretched and modified by three somewhat independent feedback cycles. Now I will make a statement that may surprise, and perhaps even disturb, some technical analysts. I think the technical analysis is mainly useful for predicting only the price movements caused by the action of the three feedback cycles, namely short-term, medium-term, and long-term feedback cycles. For this reason, I think analysts who use only technical analysis to predict big markets, highs, and lows, do not apply the discipline well. In my opinion, any effort to use technical analysis beyond its appropriate time interval carries the subject beyond what it can achieve. (The only exception to this rule, I think, is when high readings on investor sentiment exist simultaneously with extreme levels of public stock speculation.)

Many traders would say that I'm wrong, pointing out the technical deterioration that existed before many people support the markets, as proof that technical signals can anticipate them. I do not deny it. However, I believe that these technical indicators were unable to distinguish whether the market was unstable and ready for correction of three to six months or whether a significant market for bulls or bulls was imminent. In the cases cited, I believe that the indicators measured the instability that eventually transformed, for economic reasons, a long-term market, up or down. If a decline lasts more than nine months and turns into a big bear market, there must be an economic reason - the basis for a decline of this magnitude and duration.

BASIS OF TECHNICAL ANALYSIS

The Market Technicians Association (MTA) website (www.MTA- USA.org) lists more than 100 technical indicators of all types. Some 10 or 20 indicators correspond to different types of volume measurements, 20 or 30 measure different periods of the lead decline line, etc. You can assume that indicators measure many kinds of ideas, but the technical analysis has only four or five basic ideas. The different indicators are just different ways to measure these four or five basic concepts.

Highlight the divergence

Almost all technical analyzes are associated with a divergence in one way or another. Divergence occurs when two things that act together in a certain way begin to act separately or differently. In technical analysis, unless there is a discrepancy, there is no signal. Almost all the technical tools used, except the theory of the opposite opinion, are based on a kind of divergence.

Dow's original theory in the late 1900s was essentially a theory of divergence. One hundred years ago, Charles Dow postulated that this was a negative indication when Dow's industrial average reached new highs, but average transportation was not tracking. This divergence of activity is the basis of Dow's theory. The idea of divergence is found throughout the technical analysis. If I had to check, I think that over 80% of the indicators on the MTA site measure some discrepancy.

For example, one of the most fundamental technical principles, referenced more than any other (except for the contrary view), is when the expected line of decline deviates from large-cap indices. The expected decline line is the continuous sum of the number of stocks growing each day minus the declining number. Generally, this line moves, as well as the various price indices. Sometimes, however, after a long time, it peaks and never goes beyond that, although price indices do. This is the point of divergence. If this divergence continues for a few months, it is a sign of a weak and unstable market.

Many excellent books on technical analysis explain the different indicators and the ideas on which they are based. An essential point, however, is rarely addressed: how to determine if the technical indicator indicates strength or weakness in the short, medium, or long term? For example, how do you determine if the divergence of the first decline line indicates a short-term or long-term decline?

An important principle: time invariance

In 1973, I formulated a principle that has served me well over the years. I call this the principle of invariance in time. I've never tasted it; I do not know if other people had the same idea, or if modern technical work is taking care of it, and I've never seen it in the books I read. This is a principle very similar to the concept behind fractals. The principle is as follows: in technical analysis, what is true in the long run is true in the short term.

This principle means that in the technical analysis, if a certain sequence of events usually occurs in large part of the upper or lower market, you will find the same sequence, although small, before a short-term market top or bottom. For example, in a bull market, the total volume of the market generally peaks before the stock price, usually about four months earlier. You will find that the volume also reaches its maximum before the price in a move that lasts only four weeks. In this case, however, the peak occurs five or six days before the price spike. Everything is reduced in terms of time, but the sequence is the same.

The model we present is that the stock price is a modified fair value that is stretched by three feedback cycles. Each feedback loop can result in exaggerated price movements in your time. If you are trying to forecast prices in the short term, use the same scaled technical tools for the timescale. In other words, you do not need different technical tools to predict movements of different sizes; shorten the period of the tool.

For example, when measuring volume, a short-term operator can use a moving average of volumes per hour to compare. An intermediary can use a daily moving average, and a long-term investor can use the weekly volume. This principle says that, regardless of the time scale, everyone would look for the same pattern or divergence on this time scale.

In my opinion, the fact of not knowing or not understanding this principle is at the origin of some of the distortions caused by the technicians of the market. They are confused with the time referenced by the technical indicator they are looking at. This is also valid when comparing the different characteristics between markets and market funds. The technical differences between long-term funds and long-term funds are the same differences that distinguish funds and funds in the short term.

The two categories of technical indicators

We can classify technical indicators into two types. I call the first type of transition indicator and the second, a confirmation indicator. The first indicator attempts to pinpoint the exact ups and downs of the market - transition points in which the market is changing. The other type of indicator does not look for funds or funds in the market but defines when a market trend has been established, confirming when a new trend is at stake. Confirmation indicators send signals after the up or down has been created. The reason for this is to let the market go up or down and then follow the trend.

You can correctly classify the indicators as either: does it mark a transition point (up or down) or does it react after a peak or a low, confirming a market that has established a trend? Remember that these two approaches are always in conflict. A transition indicator, like the opposite view, always looks better at the worst point of the market trend. Keep them separate in your mind; your goals and objectives are completely different.

Understand the difference between market tops and bottoms

From a technical point of view, the ups and downs of the market behave differently, and you use different technical tools for each. The tops are usually long, coarse, rounded (think of an open fan), to the point where it often requires much efforts to discover the exact top. The summit seems to be scattered and seems to be more of a process than an event. The socks are different. The stockings are generally short, finish quickly, and are easy to locate. They are more of an event than a process.

It is important to realize that these are just the usual forms of ups and downs; otherwise, you may not recognize something because a fixed idea prevents you from considering it. This is what happened to many analysts in 1982. The 1982 low-market fund was not a normal event. The lower part did not appear suddenly in one day but was prolonged for six months in the bottom of compression. In Figure below, you can see the process of squeezing the number of hired actions that has reached new lows as the market has been working less. I started to see evidence of what was happening in the late spring of 1982, about three months before the last final. When I saw what was happening, watching the market complete the process, and creating the fund was like looking at a play in three acts: the bottom part was in the final act. Supporting the idea that the decline only ends at a peak prevented many technicians from realizing that it was a process fund and not an event fund, although the evidence was there.

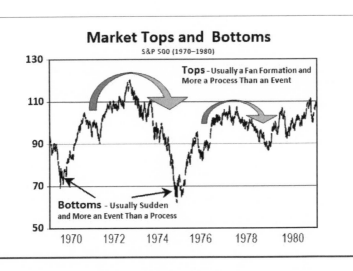

In technical analysis, the underlying idea is that in any bull market or major price movement, there is a normal sequence of events that occur internally in the market during the bidding process. What do I mean internally? Earlier on, I presented the analogy of statistical mechanics in physics with the movement of many stocks on the stock market. It is easier to predict the entire stock market than to predict individual action, just as it is easier to predict the general movement of all gas molecules relative to the movement of an individual molecule. By internal market, I intend to look at and categorize statistically what the individual stocks that make up the entire market do.

To understand this, remember that the market is the average of all stocks. The S & P 500, for example, is the average price activity of the 500 largest stocks. It all drive down to a single number, but it's a one-dimensional view. When the S & P 500 is up, it does not mean that all 500 stocks are up; It simply means that a mathematical average of 500 is on the rise. But there are a variety of different home markets that can calculate the same number.

Let me clarify that. Suppose, in two consecutive days, the S & P 500 increases by 1%. Of this number, the two days are similar. If we analyzed a little and statistically measure what the individual components were doing, we could see a different picture. Maybe in a day, only 20 of the 500 stocks are on the rise, but these 20 are up and the other 480 down, but down slightly. On the second day, all 500 stocks are up, but all are a bit high. The two days produce the same average mathematical gain of 1% and are similar from the outside, but a personal appearance presents a completely different picture. Therefore, technicians always look at the market for the domestic market.

They look at the number of stocks that are reaching new heights and new lows as major market indices move up. They also analyze the number of future actions compared to those in decline. They are looking for differences. For example, it is not a good sign to see more equities reach new lows than new highs, while major indices are reaching record highs. Similarly, it is not a good sign to see the contraction of the total volume as prices reach new heights.

Recognize a normal market cycle

What happens internally in a normal market cycle? Usually, at the beginning of a breakthrough, most stocks go up together. The model continues for a while. That's good, and that's how it should be.

This trend is measured by the width of the market. The scope of the market measures the number of stocks that are increasing daily compared to the number that is decreasing. It does not matter how much n action has advanced or decreased; a 1/8 point lead is as important as a 10 point lead. Any action that advances is an action that advances. If market averages are on the rise, technicians like to see a good width, in which the number of stocks going up is a significant number, not a small number.

History teaches us something. Usually, as the stock market expires, the averages continue to rise, but the number of stocks involved is smaller, meaning that investors are beginning to reduce their concentration. Some actions go up a lot, while many others languish or fall a little. It's not good

The volume of transactions also stops growing and begins to decline as the averages reach their peak. Usually, at the beginning of a movement, the volume of transactions increases continuously. At a certain point, the market reaches new heights, but the volume shrinks. This creates a discrepancy between volume and price.

The discrepancy is a sign that the hedging process has begun. Remember, markets are generally large, rounded, and more of a process than an event. Different stocks and different groups of stocks are often bred at different times. Several market divergences are a sign that this is happening. The problem is that the process can take a long time. There is no special way of knowing how long the process will take - it may take two months or two years. It is common to have a bearish position two or three times before the decline begins.

Making Top

As I mentioned earlier, in the market hedging process, some events usually occur before the overall averages become high (Figure 4.5). First, with the market on the rise, the number of stocks reaching new highs is at a record high. In other words, even as market averages rise and continue to reach new heights, the real number of stocks reaching new heights does not increase.

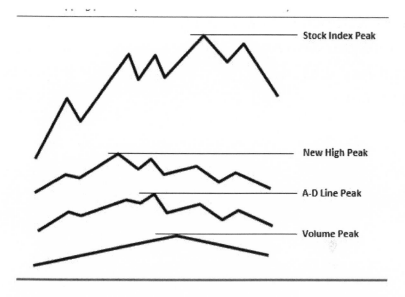

Stock Index Peak

New High Peak

A-D Line Peak

Volume Peak

Second, as the popular averages remain at new highs, the expected decline line, which is the difference between the number of shares outstanding and the number declining, does not confirm (i.e., create no new record). This defines the popular technical indication of the divergence between the expected line of decline and the popular averages.

Finally, the daily volume of trade does not increase, which is the third divergence. As the bull market continues, the volume of trade generally increases. At some point, prices continue to rise, but the volume of business is steadily growing and shrinking. This can happen for a time without cause for concern, but if it continues, it is usually the last important indication that the hedging process is nearing completion. Thus, the long-standing observation that price follows volume.

Where is the top? It is spread over time and occurs from the beginning at different times for different stocks. Many actions have increased along with the number of new highs. Other inventories increased in line with the expected decline in the line. Still, others will reach their highs once averages are reached. The action of different storage groups at the top at different times corresponds to the training of the fans, to the hedging process I referred to earlier. It is important to note that the process generally follows this path, but there are so many variations that variations are the rule.

The toping often starts at the fourth wave

From my experience in many markets, the topping process usually begins at the fourth wave of the Elliott wave movement, especially if it is a complex horizontal motion.

For the moment, let's say that every great advance happens in three slits separated by two setbacks. Pressure waves are called waves one, three and five;

the setbacks of the separation are waves two and four.

Sometimes, if the first two waves in advance are bulky and durable, the second correction, wave four, is often long and very complex. When the fourth wave is time-consuming and complex, the discrepancies mentioned usually start at the top of the third wave and not at the top of the fifth wave, which is the peak of the main indices. If this happens, the divergence persists well before the beginning of the fifth wave.

This event is the cause of more prognostic errors on the part of the technicians of the market. I have seen it several times that I came looking for it as a market indicator itself. Here is what happens:

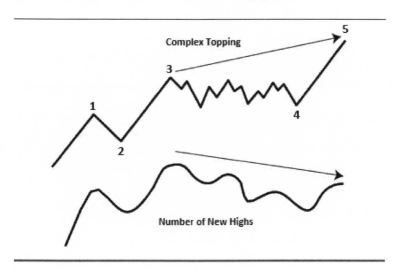

When the market moves towards a complex wave with four waves, it gives the impression of starting to circulate. Remember that a complex wave of four waves usually occurs after strong waves one and three, a short wave of two corrections separating them. Some people start to be nervous after this great race and are ready to react. They begin to perceive technical divergences as the corrective wave of four forms. At this point, the technicians usually call the summit.

As the market evolves, forming wave four, more and more people are starting to take a pessimistic position, waiting for the market to break down. Every small drop in the complex wave generates the hope that this decline is expected and that, even if the market seems weak, each decline is unexpectedly interrupted, and the market picks up a bit.

The market then moves slowly towards the previous peaks, but it looks very weak. The volume is low. Suddenly, prices reach new heights, and a strong record begins. The last wave five started. For a short time, the line of early decline comes back to life, seems solid, and the technical factors seem to be on the move. At this point, most analysts quickly return to the optimistic view, often stating that the discrepancies were a false signal. They were not; they were a bit early. It is at this stage that, faced with the optimism of investors and analysts, you should start to become very pessimistic.

Now, psychology comes in. Many investors will find that they have psychologically blocked themselves. After being out of business for a while, admitting a mistake and regaining optimism, they are now very hesitant to become pessimistic and pessimistic, even if prices start to fall. They are afraid to take a bearish position again. As prices begin to fall - in other words, prices are what people originally thought - they are somewhat stuck in an optimistic attitude because of their reluctance to reverse the situation.

One of the most important lessons a professional needs to learn is to be able to change your mind when you need to. You must be willing to admit that you were wrong. This is an example of how you can be right in the market, but you're right too early, which can ruin everything. Survival in the marketplace is often simply maintaining confidence in one's judgment.

Making bottom

Market bottoms are distinguished from market peaks from a technical point of view. Very few technical indicators, aside from market sentiment, are useful for attracting a fund. Unless it is a very rare compression fund (as in 1982), most funds end up as a kind of climax. A highlight is a type of market fund in which the sale of panic occurs in large volumes, with prices in total collapse. The culmination a few days ago, and, as the decline continues, the volume of inventories increases as prices collapse and panic occurs.

The actual end, or the bottom, usually occurs in a day. What happens is that prices collapse in large quantities than in the middle of the trading day, in the opposite direction and up, also in large quantities. This reversal disappears after a few days, after which the prices enter a long and quiet period during which nothing happens, and the volume becomes extremely light. The market seems dead, but the decline is over. During the peak of sales, it is best not to search for the fund. Take a step back or, if you invest and think it's early enough, sell it and redeem it later. Let the market make the climax and perform its opposite turnaround.

When the rally ends, it almost always decreases by at least 50% or more of the rally. During this retreat, the volume usually dries to almost zero; is death after the climax. At the moment, the market seems very weak, and there seems to be no reason to get up so early. The measures of investor sentiment are extremely negative. Investors generally expect further price declines. The most optimistic discourse is that the market will need a lot of confidence before something positive happens. You have your chance! At this point, it is often prudent to buy long-term, and you will not have to wait as long as you deem necessary.

The pivotal point

A pivotal point is essentially a price or a moment in which you will soon know which side the market will go. The problem is that one crucial point for me is not a crucial point for another person. The location of the point will depend on the model you use to understand the market.

Crossing a trend line in a price chart is an example of a central point: it represents a clear threshold when the market trend has been broken, or a new trend has been started. The reason why an essential point is so valuable is that it allows a professional to know when a company is wrong with as little loss as possible. This is especially true if the trade is long term. Suppose the market rises and threatens to exceed a long-term downtrend line. Then it breaks and increases in volume. The investor assumes a position. The chances are that the market may fall back, but if it's the real thing, it should not break again below the line. If this happens, it should be sold with a small loss. If this happens as expected, the person has entered into a long-term transaction at a very favorable starting point, with very little risk.

If the market fails and the loss is made, the investor may feel bad about the loss. Not me I understand that this was an opportunity to make a big gain, and I tested the waters with a minimum of losses. This time it was a loss; next time will probably not be. Remember that any exchange is just an exchange worth a thousand over time. Never put everything, mentally or emotionally, into one company.

I noticed something about the crucial points for many years. That's it: sometimes the stock market can become very indecisive. Volatility decreases, and the market does not seem to have direction. As this continues, more and more people are starting to realize the lack of direction. This lack of direction generally manifests itself in the three temporal domains, in the short, medium, and long term.

When that happens, you start to realize that everyone and I mean everyone, is starting to think of ever-shrinking price movements to resolve indecision or look at the microscope in a newspaper to come to solve the uncertainty. When an ad arrives, the answer is usually huge, as investors view the result as a resolution of the independent. This is rarely the case. Be careful, when it looks like all Wall Street is looking for a short-term event or information to tell them what will happen in the long run. These widely accepted central points are rarely the true ones.

Unstable markets

Unstable markets, upon which feedback cycles are about to be triggered, often share the common trait of a lack of volatility just before the reader. In my experience, the following events occur: The market will have reached a new high and seems to be holding this position very well. The discounts, when they occur, are moderate and do not seem to yield anything. These low sales often lead people to realize the strength of the market after the recent breakthrough. They say they do not seem to want to come down. Slowly, the market becomes very calm, then moves gradually to new heights at very low volume. Prices often seem to go on a ledge, slipping slowly and gaining momentum as trading volume increases. The drop often surprises people. The stock market has led investors to complacency. These falls begin with low volatility, often become very serious in price and end in high volatility.

The best indication of an unstable and volatile market is low volatility, low volume, and extreme optimism or low investor confidence. (You will see the importance of feeling in the next chapter, which deals with the theory of the contrary opinion). It is normal for extreme sentiment to be extremely low when the market experiences a sharp decline and high volatility. However, if the market calms down and the feeling of decline persists, when the volume is very low, the situation is very unstable, and a significant shift is imminent (positive return). Similarly, it is normal to have a bullish feeling as prices rise and reach new heights. However, when prices stabilize at a high price, while dry volume and sentiment become extremely optimistic - be careful. It's a very weak market.

Hide the obvious

Probably more than half of the technical indicators in the market are oscillators of one type or another. I think the oscillators are overestimated. Twenty-five years ago, I used and tested hundreds; now, I never use them. I stopped because I discovered that it is a form of esoteric calculation that often prevents a person from seeing what is happening. Their use often encourages the person to market something other than what exists - a great weakness that I previously warned. I am the wisdom of a famous physicist: "Do not fall in love with beautiful mathematics." If you can not see what's happening on the market, you will not discover a deeper truth by studying an oscillator. Cannot say anything other than the original statistic on which the oscillator is based.

I know I'm very critical here, but I'm trying to make a point. For example, many oscillators are calculated from the first decline line. The expected decline line is simply the difference between the two numbers: the number of stocks increasing and the number decreasing. There is no greater truth buried in this number. The creation of the line of decline was originally intended to signal market differences, periods of rising popular averages while most stocks were down. That's all. Then people started taking the moving averages of the line. They started to subtract a moving average from another moving average and draw that line. They started adding these differences and calculating the sum. They even started looking for trend lines of this measurement.

You can see how this process can slowly remove a person from a simple and direct observation of the market. Doing this is a bit like getting a simple equation, like $1 + 1 = 2$, framing it, picking up the fifth root, and adding 3. Doing more for that number will not give you any truth greater than the equation simple original of $1 + 1 = 2$. It is not necessary that the mathematical complexity finds deep meaning in all the data, but there is none. This is not the direction to take to find out what the stock market will do.

Just looking at the declining line, I can tell you what will be the best oscillator. Oscillators are calculated from the anticipated line of decline so that they can not say anything that the line itself cannot tell you. With many oscillators, technical analysts bottle tap water, adding bells, whistles and a little mystery, and sell it as a magic potion. It's just tap water.

CHAPTER THREE: FUNDAMENTAL ANALYSIS: DIGGING DIPPER INTO THE MARKET

One hundred years ago - if you read this sentence before 2034 - Benjamin Graham and David Dodd have published a first book on the development of fundamental analysis: a book called Security Analysis. It argues for determining the value of a business using its financial statements (in particular, the balance sheet, which shows assets and liabilities, and the income statement, which shows profits and losses over some time). Later, John Burr Williams wrote The Theory of Investment Value, which calls for determining the value of a company, discounting future dividends, or simply defining a future value in today's dollars. For example, $ 200,000 per year can be worth $ 181,818 today, assuming a "discount rate" of 10% (i.e., an investment of $ 181,818 today). and a return of 10% earns $ 200,000 after one year).

Current investment models incorporate concepts from both works to assess the value of the business. Current valuation involves using financial statement data or comparable companies to assign a value to a company. This chapter introduces the important concepts of equity valuation, that is, what to look for in the companies you buy or are short. I strongly believe that it is not impossible to estimate the value of a company between 10 and 15% of its real value in a short time. The extra hours that Wall Street analysts spend on forecasting are largely aimed at improving the accuracy of their estimates.

Whether you're looking for stocks or another market, remember that you do not need an MBA or CFA designation to use fundamental analysis intelligently. Following certain practical rules and spending a little time understanding a business can significantly improve your business profits.

Assessment of a company's financial statements

So, what should you look for when a business is profitable? The most common question is, "Has the company met or exceeded expectations?" This recommendation applies to both sales and results. The higher the percentage of success, the better.

Expectations drive Wall Street. A big surprise can be a sign that analysts do not accurately project the profits of a company. A company with a rising earnings trend (a surprise of 10%, followed by 15% gains and 20% gains) often has a higher price performance than the market. On the other hand, companies whose profits are unexpected are negative. Look for a surprise in the direction in which you are negotiating. Take the case of Southwestern Energy Company, which showed a surprise with positive gains of 7.1% in September 2007, 16.7% in December 2007 and 24% in March 2008. Between December 31, 2007, and April 30, 2008, the shares of Southwestern Energy increased by 51.87%. The unexpected gain is not the only reason for the increase but suggests that something positive is forming.

The first step in analyzing the financial statements is to understand the components. Admittedly, financial statements can seem scary, not to say boring. In my opinion, looking at dry paint is more exciting than looking at a financial statement. And that's why this section is not an academic lesson in accounting. Instead, I give you a basic understanding of what constitutes financial statements and, best of all, how you can view summaries on the Internet. Wall Street analysts read hundreds of pages of financial statements before writing business reports. Fortunately, you have nothing to do to become a profitable trader.

Public companies are required to issue four principal financial statements each quarter. As a swing trader, you need to worry about only three of them.

Not just numbers: qualitative data

Fundamentalist analysis is not just about numbers. A company is more than your income, sales, etc. Would you value a company run by a known investor in the same way as a company run by your neighbor? Qualitative factors also determine whether a company's stock is a value or not.

Some qualitative factors generally shared by optimal performance stocks are:

Superior Ownership of Management: Insider trading is a sign that the leaders who run the business place their money where they are. Financial ownership also aligns the interests of shareholders with those of management. A CEO probably thinks twice before taking a stock that can bring down the stock price if he owns a good deal of the company's shares under a 401 (k) plan. Generally, the possession of at least 10% of outstanding shares is a bullish sign.

A wide gap: For hundreds of years, castles used trenches as a defense mechanism to prevent invaders from effectively invading the castle walls. An economic gap is similar: it is the degree of competitive advantage of a firm that prevents competitors from gaining market share.

Warren Buffett, respected investor and head of Berkshire Hathaway, is one of the leading advocates of the idea of "economic pits." It looks for companies that are difficult to replace because of brand loyalty or cost advantages. Moats are often established in the pharmaceutical sector because of drug patents guaranteeing that the developer of a new drug will be the only supplier of the drug for several years.

You can see the world to some extent as including companies with wide ditches and narrower ditches (called goods) - a product that you can buy anywhere, and that does not bother you much about who manufactures is a commodity. Think about salt, sugar or, increasingly, computers. Compare companies that provide these products with those with large ditches that are difficult to move. Starbucks - which Jerry Seinfeld calls the "Five Dollars" joke - can charge higher prices for coffee cups. Sometimes the gap can be the result of a technological advantage. Google, for example, was a small technology company in 1996, but had developed a search technology that surpassed the giants of Microsoft and Yahoo! In a short time, Google has gained an important position in the field of search engines and has managed to translate this market share into advertising investment.

When analyzing companies, ask yourself how difficult it would be for a company to move the business you are looking at. The harder it is to move, the bigger the gap. Positive catalysts: Catalysts help investors revalue their stocks. Successful new products (such as the Apple iPhone) and new managers (such as Mark Hurd of Hewlett-Packard) are two catalysts that encourage investors to re-evaluate stocks.

A catalyst can also come from outside of society. When a business is acquired or purchased in a sector, its competitors often see a rise in share prices when investors re-evaluate the shares based on the multiple of the purchase price used for the acquisition. Investors also expect another takeover in the sector.

Negative catalysts that can propel a company's stock down may include a loss of profit, the launch of a new product by the competitor and the resignation of key management.

How to evaluate a business based on the data you have collected

You may feel that you can seek advice from people for financial statement analysis, profit reporting review, and qualitative data evaluation, but how much is this company worth? There is no line in the financial statements stating, "This business is worth $ 5 billion." Please do not pay more than this amount.

If you bring together ten different analysts in a room and ask them to analyze a business, you will probably get ten different answers (ideally, they are at least close to each other). There are differences in the way investors value companies.

Understand the two main methods of evaluation

The two main methods of stock valuation are relative valuation models and absolute valuation models:

A relative evaluation model is probably the model you will use most often as a swing professional. Relative valuation estimates the value of a business based on peer exchanges in the market. The model can be based on earnings (using the price/earnings ratio, for example), sales (price/price ratio), book value (book-to-market price) or a dozen other indices.

By far, the price-earnings ratio (P / E) is the most common relative valuation method. For example, if Macy and Dillard exchange 12 times the profit, then maybe J.C. Penney should also. It may even be that Macy's deserves trading with a price, as its earnings are expected to grow faster in the coming years than its competitors. Or maybe J.C. Penney deserves bargain at a discount to his competitors because his net profit margin (net profit divided by sales) is lower than his competitors. You had the idea.

An absolute rating model is calculated independently of a company's peer reviews. Instead of concluding what Macy or Dillard are negotiating, an analyst who

J. C. Penney determines a value based on the company's earnings, cash flow, or dividends. Business valuation differences mainly result from deviations from forecasts of future results. If it were possible to know for sure what a company would do in the next ten years, there would be little disagreement about the value of the business today.

RESEARCHING COMPANIES BASED ON ITS FOUNDATIONS

You can identify ground negotiations (and technology for that purpose) in two ways: starting with the security market and exploring promising industries or identifying candidates with promising local characteristics. One approach is from top to bottom while the other is from the bottom up. Both ways have merit.

This section describes how to identify promising candidates to buy or reduce using a top-down or bottom-up approach - and how to determine which approach is best for you.

See the forest for trees: the top-down approach

The top-down approach identifies promising candidates for the derivatives market, starting with market analysis (stock markets, commodities, foreign exchange markets, etc.). Then, it is divided into specific sectors before finally examining the individual titles. This approach implicitly has more weight in the markets and industries at the expense of the merits of a sole proprietorship, as these larger elements are more important in determining the return of security than factors at the firm level. A top-down trader cares less if he or she swings with XYZ Oil Company or ABC Oil Company (depending on the individual characteristics of each company) and more if he negotiates a stock of energy or drugs.

The top-down approach allows you to understand the state of the market in general, which is valuable because most stocks follow general market trends. For example, if the stock market is ugly and reaches new lows every two or three weeks, your negotiations will be ineffective. On the other hand, if you eagerly reduce all stocks that evolve as the market reaches new heights, you'd better prepare yourself for unpleasant losses.

Using this approach, you begin to assess whether the global market is overvalued, devalued, or simply correct. So you ask if the sector is likely to outperform or underperform. Finally, you examine individual security to see if your statistics are impressive enough to justify the investment.

Top-down analysis has two specific steps:

1. Determine if the world market price is correct.

This step allows you to determine if the global market is cheap or cheaper. So you know if you have to trade long or short. As a swing trader, you do not have the time to call analysts, search government data, and create a business model that perfectly captures all the information that can affect a market in general. Even if you have time for all this, I have never seen the evidence that such complexities improve predictability (I apologize to my professor of econometrics).

2. Assess the perspectives of the different industries of the market.

This step helps you focus on promising or backward industries so that the wind is at your expense when you buy or sell bonds in this industry. If the market is overvalued, for example, which industries have the greatest downside opportunities? Being right in the global market and the bad market in the industry can leave you helpless.

The Bottom-Up Approach: Starting from the Grassroots Level

The bottom-up approach is different from the top-down approach I described earlier in this chapter. Instead of starting with the global stock market and switching to the industrial group, the bottom-up approach places less emphasis on global business cycles, from company to company. Whether you prefer a fundamental analysis of technical analysis or you are looking for long and promising candidates in a weak market (or weak in a strong market), you can favor the bottom-up approach from top to bottom.

The bottom-up approach usually begins with a kind of screen, which you use to identify promising candidates, long and short. Some screens are very liberal: they generate dozens of possible candidates, which reduces the time you can devote to anyone. The other screens are very conservative - the criteria used are so strict that you can only have five or six possible candidates to evaluate. Think about using a screen based on fundamentals such as sieving gold. A lot of waste involves these valuable nuggets, and your job is to find them in the middle of all the trash.

In the following sections, I show you how to do just that.

Use screens to filter information

Fundamental screens can take everything into account, from the earnings growth rates to the average daily volume, to the changes in the analyst's estimate. Sometimes this variety leads to an overflow of information, which can be discouraging if you use the first screen for the first time. Fortunately, when you create your screen using the criteria you want to focus on, you do not have to worry about the ready and informative lots that vendors are selling to the public.

In addition to covering the general selection criteria, I look at two screens on the long side: a growth screen and a value screen. I show you what criteria you need to consider for each screen type to effectively screen. Note: These screens are only for illustration to guide the development of your screens.

Take advantage of the value and growth screens of your swing trading. When growth exceeds value

81

stocks, use the growth screen. And when the value is what's inside, focus on the value screen. Determine what to expect by plotting a ratio graph of a growth and value index.

Note the marked differences in yields. During the five years ended December 31, 2006, the Russell 1000 Growth Index generated an annualized return of 10.86% compared to the Russell 1000 Growth index's (large-cap growth) 2.69% return. If you convert the annualized return (which looks like an average return for the period) into a total return (while the index has increased in total over the five years), the numbers are even more surprising: 45% over five years, while the high-growth growth index increased by 14.19%.

What you need to know about basic selection criteria

Before you start using screens, note that the value and growth screens usually have similar characteristics. For example, both screens should exclude low-priced securities and rarely-traded securities. When looking for long-term candidates, they must include a high-yield equity field.

The main difference between value and growth screens is that growth screens tend to focus on areas of earnings growth rate, while value stocks focus on valuation metrics such as the P / L indices, some fields differ between the two. For example, low-priced stocks are often identified using the price/sales ratio. Growth stocks are rarely found using this measure.

Do not let it surprise you if you see the same fields in the growth and value stocks with different filter values. For example, the return on equity criteria is present on the value and growth screens because the return on equity is an important measure for all companies you buy or sell. The higher this statistic, the more the company can benefit from every dollar of capital.

When entering your selection criteria, be careful not to be in the liberal or conservative extreme. You want your screen to capture businesses from multiple industries, not just one in these challenging times. If the members of an industrial group dominate a screen, one of their criteria will probably be very strict. But you do not need all sectors to be represented to have a good screen. When an industry is going through a difficult period, it can be understood that few members of this group, if any, appear on screens identifying potential buyers.

When growth is on the rise

Important criteria to include in a growth screen include:

A stock price measure: This number allows you to exclude negotiated shares of less than an amount you enter, for example, $ 5 per share.

Average daily volume: This part of the screen avoids securities that trade a few hundred shares a day and are therefore difficult to enter or exit. There is no doubt that these bonds offer opportunities, but I do not think the return potential will outweigh the risk.

Growth stocks generally reside in the technology, health, and consumer discretionary sectors, but may also reside in other parts of the market.

The following factors characterize growing businesses:

• Earnings growth rate above the market average (for example, above 25%)

• Sales growth rate above the market average (above 10%)

• New products and new management Low or no dividend payout

• High price/reserve ratios higher than the average price/earnings ratio

Use the growth screen when growth exceeds value stocks. When creating your growth screen, make sure you only have a few companies to work with, but not too restrictive to exclude potential opportunities.

Use a growth screen to find fast-growing companies

Growth stocks show high earnings growth rates. Therefore, the next growth screen, which can be implemented with the most popular filtering programs, focuses on earnings growth recently and historically. Although the method of enabling these filtering functions depends to a large extent on the filtering program you are using, I recommend that you always enter these numbers:

Last closing price ≥ $ 5: I consider the shares below $ 5 as shares listed in cents.

Average daily volume (last 50 days) ≥ 100,000 shares: Unless you trade $ 5 million or more, the average daily volume of 100,000 shares with a market value of $ 5.00 or more should allow you to enter and exit without much difficulty.

Earnings per share growth (last quarter vs. last quarter) ≥ 25%: This is the value recommended by William J. O'Neil, founder of Investor's Business Daily.

Earnings Per Share (EPS) growth rate greater than or equal to 10%: O'Neil also recommends this figure.

Relative Strength Index ≥ 80: other value recommended by the founder of Investor's Business Daily.

Return on equity ≥ 18%: In my experience, 18% is the minimum return on equity I would look for in the companies I want to manage in the long term.

I consider these criteria important in growth stocks. The first two fields ensure that you look at the net shares traded above $ 5 per share, which excludes cents from your analysis. The next two are profit growth rates - the lifeblood of the growth stock. The fifth area examines price performance relative to the global market. (The growth stocks you buy must be in the top 20% of the market.) The final criterion, return on equity, limits your universe of analysis to well-managed companies, which means that not necessarily for fundamentals Of the industry.

Evaluate your screening results

Once your screen is complete, you need a ranking system that allows you to focus on the most promising candidates and lower your path. You can rank stocks based on their P / E indices, for example, from lowest to highest, if you are looking for swing trading candidates on the longest side of the market. You can also sort bonds based on their return on equity or price to free up cash flow indices. The ranking helps you push the cream to the top.

HGS Investor allows users to create "combined rankings" that allow classification based on two or more metrics (such as 30% weighting in the EPS classification and 70% in the P / E).

By identifying a promising candidate for swing trading using the first screen, the proper security should jump you on. You should not have to make too many misunderstandings or questions. Here's how to analyze your results:

If you want to keep security for a long time, make sure it generates strong earnings, low valuation, and strong performance.

If you prefer to reduce security, make sure that earnings growth, valuation, and the performance sector are not satisfactory.

Decide which approach to use

Which approach should you use? Even if you hate it, this question does not have a correct answer. The chosen approach depends solely on your trading style. Would you prefer to identify mature industries ready to take off? If so, use the descending approach. Do you like to develop screens and then examine the filtered results for promising candidates? In this case, use the ascending approach.

Investors based on fundamentals are generally downward. Swing operators and technical operators are often descendants. However, an operator based on fundamental principles can be descendant, and a technical swing operator can be upward. Remember, there is no good or bad way. Promising candidates are the ones you find, whether you start with a top-down or bottom-up approach.

Ideally, a security that you find using the bottom-up approach can also be found using a top-down approach. But the simultaneous use of both approaches is complex and time-consuming. Choose one and follow it to identify promising areas that are perfect (if you are the top-down type) or stocks that are undervalued or overvalued at the base level (if you are the bottom up kind of person).

CHAPTER FOUR: DEVELOPING AND IMPLEMENTING YOUR TRADING PLAN

How to develop simple balance sheet trading strategies lays the foundation for the development of short- and medium-term trading strategies. We will start by discussing swing trading objectives and then follow some of the recommended steps to develop a strategy from scratch.

We will not discover any Holy Grail, but we hope that the steps and structure described in this article will provide a responsible path for creating a strategy to call yours.

WHY DEVELOP A NEGOTIATING STRATEGY IN THE FIRST PLACE?

As fun as it is to get up every morning and decide in advance which titles to exchange, the direction in which to exchange them, the sign of entry, etc., are not realistic.

I'm sure some people shoot freely, but in this case, I think trading would be a hobby more fun than serious.

To achieve and make sure to be consistent, we must develop a strategy or set of rules that we will follow each day. By executing our rules, we can document our results, check performance, and identify what works and does not work.

Make no mistake; profitable business strategies are not something you will spontaneously write an afternoon in your free time. Business strategies will require deliberate thinking and creativity to find (the best, at least).

After all, our market advantages are defined by the trading strategy, advantages which are hard to find.

STEP 1 - BUILD THE FOUNDATION OF YOUR TRADING STRATEGY

We know that our goal is to capture a movement of several days or weeks in the market. Now we must find a repeatable model and measure its profitability.

The simpler and more direct your rules, the more solid and sustainable your strategy will be.

Simple and straightforward is not always the most cost-effective solution, but it's also great when you're running a live strategy and trying to find out if it's working as expected when you're downgraded.

There are a million ways to create rules for a strategy and the scope of this article, click our fingers, and create them using price action and some moving averages.

If you have niche models that you have observed on many occasions, the best way to collect data on possible input/output signals is to retrospectively examine these events and analyze their exact origin and evolution.

ACTION OF PRICE AS OUR SAMPLE FRAMEWORK

In any period, in any market, we can create a set of rules to classify price movement as a trend or interval limit.

When a market is in trend, the chart starts somewhere in the lower left corner of the screen and goes up in the upper right corner of the screen.

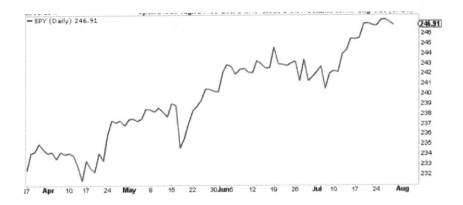

Trends are characterized by different rates of change and varying degrees of setback along the way, but overall, a movement from the bottom left to the top right is the "norm."

When a market is limited to the limit, it means that a trend does not exist.

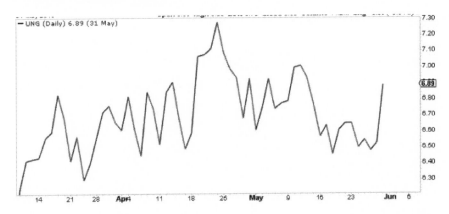

The chart should depict a market that is moving sideways with choppy price action and no clear winner (sellers or buyers) in control.

There are several ways to create a rule-based definition to classify these price action states. Some examples may include the use of:

• Moving Averages.

• Price structure (higher highs and higher lows).

• Lookback returns (are we higher than we were there are X measures?).

• Technical patterns and geometric shapes.

The great novelty in identifying these types of market environments is that once a market is trending, it tends to persist in that state.

The same applies to markets with range limits. Most leaks will fail, and the market will tend to return to average until this does not happen again.

STEP 2 - CREATION OF TRADING STRATEGY RULES

When the market changes, we have a consistent direction. As tempting as the short signals seem to be in an uptrend, we want to avoid distractions and focus only on trading in the direction of the trend.

So the question is, how do we capture some of this movement in a positive and expected (risk-adjusted) way?

In retrospect, the answer to this question is to buy and keep, duh! Unfortunately, the markets are not always so generous; we had no idea that this trend would persist as long in real time.

Take a closer look at how the price tends to increase a race from one to two weeks, then enter a consolidation period of the same duration before starting your next move.

Using these observations and exploiting what we know about trends, we can define some rules for a trading strategy (in the real world, you will probably start with something other than observations):

• Wait until the end of the 20 EMA period (yellow line).

• Buy the first bar that closes above 20EMA AND the highest bar of the previous day.

• Stop at 1 ATR below the entry price (or below the previous minimum, whichever is higher).

• Take out half of the exchange on a multiple of 1.5X ATR.

• Leave the rest with a lock lower than the previous three days minimum.

We could call this a strategy of withdrawal of the stock price uptrend.

Note that we define an entry, profit, and exit condition. We have also included some of the risk management using an initial stop-loss.

Also, logic and rules are simple and robust:

• Only target bullish stocks and trade exclusively in this direction.

• Make use of a predefined stop loss to limit losses.

• Get partial profits with 1.5X multiple risks to reduce the number of saw blades and smooth the equity curve.

• Leave the remaining half of the business as far as the trend allows, to maximize profits.

STEP 3 - BACKTEST TRADING STRATEGY

So, did we end our trend-setting strategy? Have we discovered the Holy Grail? Unfortunately no. Although this strategy was excellent for the Priceline example above, it must be tested on more than one event.

The next stage in our strategy development process would be to apply the same set of rules to more stocks and periods. This is commonly known as backtesting, which Investopedia has defined as:

Backtesting is the method of testing a trading strategy against relevant historical data to ensure its viability before the trader puts real capital in jeopardy. Trading of a strategy can be simulated by a trader over an appropriate period and analyze the results in terms of profitability and risk levels.

The backtesting process is something that deserves a whole blog post because of the many pitfalls that a trader can fall through by this process.

We will not cover these details for the scope of this book, but at a great level, the aim is to validate your strategy on all of the sample data and sample that you can obtain.

Some quick tips:

Do not forget to take into account the costs of slippage and commission.

Test different market regimes. For example, a simple follow-up test from 2009 to 2017 puts you in a bull market. If a 20-day moving average gives good results, but 18, 19 and 21-day moving averages have radically different performance, be very careful.

As a result, you may discover that the original settings that you started with do not last in time and that it may be a 10-period EMA with a 2X ATR loss better modeled in the function of adjusted return to risk.

Finally, you want to validate the robustness of your rules, making the necessary adjustments, but most importantly, you do not want to adjust too much the rules and parameters, because you run the risk of adapting your strategy to your dataset.

STEP 3B - YOU MUST BACKTEST EQUIVALENTS FOR DISCRETIONARY TRADERS

The Discretionary trading systems that rely on variable inputs and their dynamic weighting will not be able to quantify their rules fully and will, therefore, participate in the traditional backtesting steps described above.

The closest equivalent is to establish a history and document your results live.

This can mean paper-based transactions for a few weeks, months, or even a year until you have enough confidence and the size of your sample to make sure your trading methodology is profitable.

It can be argued that the paper trade does not bring about the financial and emotional consequences of real money trading. A more realistic history would, therefore, use real money, but small. It was my approach when I created my swing trading system.

I started to risk 0.25 to 0.30% for trading for a whole year. My second year, I increased my trading risk to 0.5% and the third year, and at the current level, I risk up to 1% per transaction.

Starting small, I was able to discover the holes in the system, make the necessary adjustments along the way, and slowly maximize the risk I was taking. It took me nearly three years to reach the "real size," but over the years, I gained a lot of experience building confidence in my system and understanding its risk profile in various environments.

STEP 4 - GO LIVE OR START OVER

Once your backtesting is over, you should have a good idea if the strategy you set for negotiating is worth it. Keep in mind that a profitable backtest does not guarantee that your system will work this way in the future.

If you have not found something that generates favorable returns, you must again resist the temptation to make adjustments and constant adjustments to the parameters of a strategy to integrate them into the dataset.

The same risks we discussed earlier overeating can be very dangerous. It is, therefore, generally advisable to start with a new strategic foundation, rules, etc.

STEP 5 - ENHANCED MAINTENANCE AND STRATEGY

If you have reached Step 5 with a trading strategy on the road, generating profits and tracking your backtest profile, congratulations!

This is good news. The bad news is, it does not mean you can sit back and wait for your profits to continue to turn.

Market conditions are constantly changing; new entrants are entering the market; others are coming out, which means that your trading system may lose their edge over time.

To fix this, you need to monitor your system continually and see if everything works as your backtest, and your live trading experience suggest.

Sooner or later, you are prone to face a longer demotion than you are used to, or unexpected events will occur on the market, which will make you wonder if the system is still working as originally planned.

When you start to doubt your system, the best question is:

Does my system work as expected, given current market conditions (inputs)?

If, for example, your system is malfunctioning in low volatility environments and we are suddenly facing a long period of low market volatility, unsatisfactory results are to be expected.

There is nothing wrong with your system; it's just not the ideal environment.

On the contrary, if your system is historically successful in bull markets and you are faced with an abnormally large loss in an uptrend, it is time to analyze what is happening carefully.

TRADING IS NOT ALWAYS SMOOTH

It would be good for our trading accounts to pay constant weekly dividends for all our hard work, but unfortunately, that is not the case. The truth is that most trading strategies offer unequal returns, are probably not correlated with the S & P500 and will make us more disappointed than ever.

Trend tracking strategies have well-documented return profiles with exactly this value.

It's easy to accept this by reading it in a blog post, but try to set up a strategy and introduce yourself to the day of collection # 137 while the S & P500 reaches new heights, and your guru of trading on social networks publishes how non-profits stop entering

I guarantee you that the only thought you have is:

What shit! I need to find something new.

It is strongly recommended to resist this temptation to abandon the ship to adopt a new trading strategy. If I look at the results of my business for the calendar year 2016, only two months of this year accounted for 80% of my profits. This means that ten months have passed without the needle being moved in one way or another.

As long as your system is working as expected, given market conditions, do not save it so quickly.

TRADING MANAGEMENT AND POSITION SIZING IS KING

Risk management and sizing positions are probably the closest things we can get from a holy grail in the trade. The most effective strategies in the world can become disastrous in the hands of an irresponsible or overly aggressive professional. Also, too much risk aversion can be equally detrimental from opportunity cost.

There are many principles and common sense rules to apply when thinking about risk management, but the specific limits vary considerably depending on the operator.

For instance, a 21-year-old trader, fresh out of college with a $ 12,000 trading account, can probably explain the risk of 2% of his trading account.

On the other hand, a 55-year-old executive with a $ 1 million trading account probably should not even have all that capital in one strategy, let alone risk 1 to 2 percent of their total account per transaction.

STRENGTHENING YOUR DEFENSE: POSITION SIZE AND RISK MANAGEMENT

Row size and risk management go hand in hand. These are the two most important things to consider before you even start trading. While most fresh traders think that "winning" is what trade means, they will soon realize that losing is much more common. The fact about trading is that you will probably end the month or the year with more losing trades than winning trades. That's why risk management is so important in the negotiations. The idea of our strategy is to allow a winning negotiation to pay off and pay for several losing deals. The only way to do this is to have a certain risk by limiting your losses and allowing your winning offers to compensate.

Position size:

If I had to do it, I would say that the size of the job is something the newcomers do not even think about. This is a subject that is often overlooked by new traders. The size of the appropriate position varies from one trader to another and may depend on the size of your account. Although the new operator must use a maximum size to avoid catastrophic failure, there is also a minimum size that will eventually lead to the same result and failure. If you are a new merchant or a merchant with a small account, this lesson is very important to you.

How much is too small?

Among the first questions, a fresh trader will ask himself is: "How much capital do I need to start trading?" Sadly, there is no correct solution to this question, and the amount of capital required will be different depending on each business idea. The first step you must achieve in calculating capital requirements starts with a good understanding of the cost of doing business. This must include the cost of the commissions charged by your broker, as well as any fees that may apply. Once we have established the cost of starting a business, we can begin to look at the risks and benefits to determine the capital needed for our business idea.

Although at first glance, it sounds ridiculous, there is very small position size. It is not uncommon for fresh entrants to make the right choice, sell more of their purchases, and end up losing money. Trading is not free, and the price negotiated may vary from one broker to another. I use Fidelity most often for my broker, who charges $ 7.95 per transaction. We make use of it as a basis for calculating costs. Now, let's say you just started, and you only have $ 500 to get started. Although it is not impossible to develop a small account, you must take into account that you will be seriously disadvantaged and that your chances of success will be zero. With smaller bills, rules and discipline are much more important.

Example

You have looked at the EST ticker (it's not a real ticker), and you start to like the price action. EST is presently trading at $ 2.50 per share. You want to start small to decide to use only $ 100.00 on your total value of $ 500. With your $ 100.00, you can buy 40 shares EST. After a few days, the stock has risen by $ 0.30 per share, and you decide it's time to get your first winning deal. After you earn $ 0.30 per share and have a total of 40 shares, you get $ 112.00, which is a return of 12%. Getting a 12% return on trade is very acceptable and even above average. Once your money has been emptied by your broker, you will realize that the value of your account has dropped by $ 4.00. You must strive to know how you have just lost money during a winning negotiation; then you will find a very high and lousy commission rate from your broker. In our scenario, we use $ 7.95 as a cost base. Your dealer will charge you each time you buy shares, and each time you sell shares. The transaction above has returned you $ 12.00, but the commission fees associated with the transaction cost $ 16.00, leaving you with a net loss of $ 4.00. Many new operators with small accounts will be eliminated simply by commissions. That said, I strongly believe in the possibility of burning commissions to gain experience and knowledge about buying any online trading course. This size of positions is small, and you will need more capital to take advantage of this scenario.

POSITION SIZING AND RISK MANAGEMENT

Risk management:

As any successful negotiator will say that risk management is the number one rule to follow. This may require extreme discipline and may even make you miss one or two trades. This is a long term protection plan designed to keep you in the game as long as possible and provide you with the best chance of success. There is absolutely no need to complicate risk management, and we will simplify the task.

You should never risk more than 2% of your total trading capital in one transaction.

For instance, if you have a $ 600.00 trading account, you can only risk a maximum of 2% per trade on that $ 500.00. This leaves you with a risk of $ 10 per trading. It is almost impossible to risk $ 10.00 per trading. If you are considering trading with a $ 500.00 account, you may want to consider this.

SET YOUR ENTRIES AND EXITS

Merchants spend hours adjusting their entry strategies, then they blow up their accounts and have bad ones. Most of us do not have effective exit planning, often being shaken by the worst possible price. We can remedy this situation by applying conventional strategies that can increase profitability. We will begin with the misunderstood concept of market timing and then stop and implement methods that protect profits and reduce losses.

It's impossible to talk about exits without realizing the importance of a maintenance period that fits well with your trading strategy. These magical delays are roughly aligned with the overall approach chosen to withdraw money from financial markets:

• Day Trading: from minutes to hours

• Swing Trading: hours per day

• Position Trading: days to weeks

• Investment timing: weeks to months

Choose the category that best fits your market approach, as it determines how much time you need to record your profits or losses. If you stick to the parameters, you could turn a business investment or dynamic movement on a scalp. This approach requires discipline because some positions work so well that you want to keep them beyond time constraints. While you can extend and shorten the waiting time to take into account market conditions, leaving the business within the boundaries of the business generates trust, profitability, and negotiation skills.

Market Timing

Make it a habit to set reward and risk goals before participating in each negotiation. Check the chart and find the next level of resistance that may occur within the time frame. This marks the target of the reward. Then find the price at which it will be proven that you are wrong if the security turns and goes down. This is your target. Now calculate the reward/risk ratio by looking at least 2: 1 in your favor. Nothing less and you should skip the trade by switching to a better opportunity.

Concentrate on managing the exchanges on the two main exit prices. Suppose everything is going well and the price in advance is close to your reward goal. The rate of price change now comes into play because the faster it reaches the magic number, the more flexibility you have to choose a favorable exit. Your first option is to become blind for the award, congratulate yourself for a job well done and move on to the next negotiation. A better option when the price tends to your advantage is to allow it to exceed the reward goal by placing a protective stop at that level when you try to increase earnings. Then search for the next obvious barrier, staying positioned as long as it does not violate your waiting period.

Slow advances are more difficult to negotiate because many bonds come together but do not reach the reward goal. This requires a profit protection strategy that comes into play once the price has covered 75% of the distance between your risk and return objectives. Place an endpoint that protects the partial winnings or, if you trade in real time, hold a finger on the exit button while watching the ticker. The trick is to stay in position until the price action gives you a reason to leave.

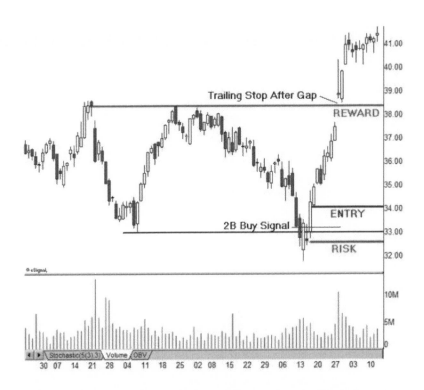

In this example, the action of Electronic Arts Inc. (EA) is sold in October, which is lower than the August minimum. It goes back two days later, emitting a Buy 2B signal, as explained in 1993 classic "Trader Vic: Processes of a Wall Street Master." The trader calculates the reward/risk as follows when planning an entry close to 34 USD and a stop loss below the new level of support:

• TARGET REWARD (38,39) - RISK TARGET (32,60) = 5.79

- REWARD = REWARD POINT (38.39) - ENTRY (34) = 4.39

- RISK = ENTRY (34) - RISK TARGET (32.60) = 1.40

- REWARD (4.39) / RISK (1.40) = 3.13

The position is better than expected, staying above the reward goal. The trader responds with a stop of profit protection just to the reward goal, increasing it every night, provided that the benefit progresses. (See also: Playing the gap.)

Stop Loss Strategies

The stops must go where you leave them when a security breach violates the technical reason for which you made the change. This is a confusing concept for operators who have learned to make stops based on arbitrary values such as a 5% or USD 1.50 discount below the entry price. These investments are meaningless because they are not in line with the features and volatility of this instrument. Instead, use technical resource violations (such as trend lines, rounded numbers, and moving averages) to establish the original price of the stop loss.

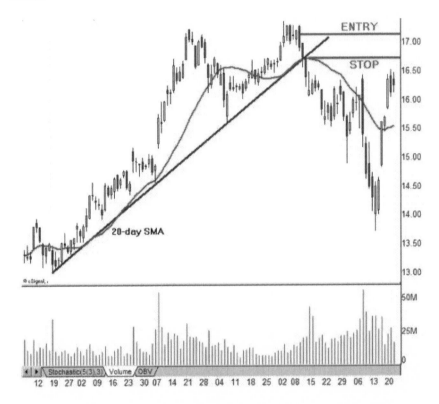

In this example, the shares of Alcoa Corporation (AA) are steadily increasing. It is above $ 17 and falls back on a three-month trend line. The next jump returns to its maximum, prompting the operator to enter a long position in anticipation of an escape. Common sense dictates that a break in the trend line proves that the rally thesis is false and requires immediate exit. Also, the 20-day simple moving average is aligned with the trendline, which increases the chances that a violation will result in additional selling pressure. (See also: The Trend Curve Utility.)

New markets require a further step in the actual placement of stops. Now, algorithms regularly target current stop loss levels, shocking retailers, and then sending back support or resistance. This requires that the stops be set aside figures that say you are wrong and you have to leave. Finding the perfect price to avoid these stopovers is more of an art than science. Typically, an additional 10 to 15 cents should operate in a low volatility market, while a push game may require an additional 50 to 75 cents. You have more options when you look in real time because you can reach your initial risk target by re-entering if the price rebounds to the disputed level.

Scaling exit strategies

Increase your break-even point when a new business becomes profitable. It can create trust because you now have free trade. So sit back and let it roll until the price reaches 75% of the distance between the risk and reward targets. You then have the option to leave at once or in pieces. This decision monitors the size of the position and the strategy employed. For example, it makes no sense to split a small business into even smaller parts. It is, therefore, more efficient to look for the most opportune moment to give up the entire participation or apply the strategy of the "stop-at-reward" strategy.

The most important positions benefit from a staggered exit strategy ranging from one third to 75% of the distance between the risk and reward targets and the second third to the target. Place a stop behind the third piece after it passes the target, using this level as an exit at the bottom of the rock if the position turns south. Over time, you will discover that this third piece is a lifeline, generating substantial profits. Finally, consider an exception to this layered strategy. Sometimes the market distributes gifts, and our job is to reap the rewards. Then, when a shock of news creates a considerable gap in your direction, get out of any position immediately and without repentance, following the old wisdom: it never looks like a gift in your mouth.

CHAPTER FIVE: WALKING THROUGH A TRADE

Here, I see the swing dealer's point of view in search of a business opportunity, and this chapter provides an example of identifying a possible trade through the eight main steps. These steps show how to integrate the concepts discussed elsewhere in this book. I use the top-down analysis framework (see Chapters 6 and 8) to identify and execute the operation, and all the data I use is actual market data. If you realize how I approach and research potential candidates to do business, you can develop the techniques that I introduce or incorporate aspects with which you agree.

Step 1: Size up the market

Mr. Market is where everything starts for the swing merchant. To be an experienced trader, you need to know the state of the stock markets, commodities, fixed income, and even currencies. Why Because these markets are related. For example, if you realize that currency prices are rising, you must be ready for a bear market price bond. Or if you find that bond prices are falling rapidly, you will probably see equity weakness. The rise in oil prices positively affects the shares of energy companies; the weakening dollar contributes to higher commodity prices; And so on. Looking at all major markets improves your trading ability by giving you an indication of the likely direction of other markets.

Since you are likely to trade in stocks, you need to take a close look at US stock markets to determine which style (growth or value) is performing well and which market cap ranges (large-cap, mid-cap or small-cap) leads the market. The best way to get this analysis is to use relative strength graphs, which are an index to each other.

Step 2: Identify key industry groups

In the example I cited in the previous section, the short-term trend is on the rise. You must, therefore, look for new positions in the market in the longer term. To do this, you need to look at the major groups in the sector. Buying shares in large groups increases the chances that your shares will increase with the general market.

You can identify key industrial groups in several ways. Investor's Business Daily publishes a ranking of all industry groups in the market. You can focus on the top 10% of the list to identify the longest values in the market.

High Stock Investor Stock (HGS Investor) is a software that provides a classification of the major groups of backward industries and allows users to map each group in the industry. Analyzing industry group charts is a step above, focusing simply on the top 10% because you can apply technical analysis.

This step tells you that you need to start your search for promising negotiations ranked by the sector in the top 10% of the longest candidates and the bottom 10% for the shortest candidates.

Now that you know which groups are in the first look for candidates in the two main industry groups: Residential / Commercial Construction and Steel Fabrication. The next section guides you through this step.

Step 3: Selection of promising candidates

It's really hard to know which industry groups to focus on. You, therefore, only cover most of your assessment in the first two steps. Your success depends more on the market you are trading and the groups of sectors you have chosen than the company you have selected in one sector.

So, how do you pick promising candidates from the market-bought side in the two industry groups mentioned in the previous section? Most swing traders primarily use technical analysis to select a value. I recommend that you first use fundamental analysis to select the most promising candidates. Then use technical analysis to time your inputs and outputs.

I want to emphasize on why taking into account the fundamentals of a business is important: even if it is simply to classify businesses in a sector according to their PEG ratios or to obtain the classification of income provided By Investor's Daily Business, HGS Investor and other products, it's best to incorporate some of the fundamental approaches into your swing trading compared to no fundamental analysis at all.

Step 4: Determine the position size

Okay, so I found my company, but how much should I spend on it? Not all of this - no one is sure of a business unless you have insider information, and even then, there is never a 100% guarantee that things will end as you wish.

Determine the size of your position by identifying your level of loss limit and limiting losses between 0.25% and 2.0% of the value of your account if security reaches this level of stop loss. For these two operations, I define the size of my position according to the level of risk. Specifically, I will calculate the number of shares I can buy from GFA and SID, assuming I make stop-loss requests below a new support level.

Step 5: Execute your order

Your order entry strategy must be consistent with your commitment to swing trading. Full-time swing traders can add an intraday trading overlay strategy to try to buy at a better price. Part-time swing traders must use threshold orders to enter near the closing price on the day the signal is generated.

I do not use a secondary exchange overlay for the simple reason that I do not want to aggregate the value to such a micro level. My outperformance (or alpha) should come to hold the trade for a few days or weeks. So I'm not so worried about security being done minute by minute as long as it's over the threshold.

With no regard to whether you are a part-time or full-time swing trader, it is extremely important to introduce stop-loss orders (until they are canceled so that they are not canceled after a day) as soon as you do your trading.

The only exception to this rule is for full-time traders who observe their positions during market hours, every day. These brokers may, if they wish, enter price alerts on their positions at the levels at which a stop loss order would be entered. Taking the SID actions from the beginning of this chapter as an example, a full-time swing trader can enter the stop loss level of $ 34.59 as the level at which he receives a TradeStation e-mail or message box. Once the alert is reached, the merchant can execute the order, possibly using a Level II course to facilitate transactions.

However, the use of such claims for mental loss has drawbacks, the main one being that the withdrawal of positions in loss is not automated. Entering a job is not as emotional as losing. When you have to sell a losing position (or cover a lost position), you can begin to doubt yourself. You can check the graph to see if the stop loss level has been set too aggressively. There may be a level of support a few points below the current price, and you would prefer to reduce the level of stop loss. And then, perhaps, as you reflect on this, realize that the price has temporarily recovered above the stop-loss level. "You see, I knew it would probably change." Before you know it, you find perfect excuses for which you should let it go further and reduce losses to another level.

That's why I prefer automated stop-loss levels. Yes, entering a stop loss level officially announces my request for everyone to see it. But I will bear this cost with the ability to let my emotions influence my exit from a lost position. The stop-loss order does its job without emotions. It runs, and you are informed.

Step 6: Recording your trade

Now that I have run my business, my next job is to register them in my trading journal. The more detailed your journal is, the more useful it will be. On the other hand, if you enter so much detail that you might be afraid to register your business, you risk not keeping your journal up to date, and the work will eventually accumulate. So, always try to find a balance.

Step 7: Monitor your shares' motion and leave promptly

After entering your positions and publishing them in your trading log, you must monitor them and focus on your exit strategy, which you must inform when you enter three scenarios:

• When the position is profitable

• When the position is not profitable

• When the position winds sideways

My exit strategy, in this example, as my entry strategy, is simple:

Ideally, I'm getting closer to the 9-day moving average. If stocks go up, closing below the nine-day average will keep me in shape.

If and when the shares reach the stop-loss level, I leave, that's all.

If the actions deviate and do nothing, I leave after ten days to be able to deploy the capital elsewhere.

To return to the examples at the beginning of this chapter, shortly after the purchase of GFA shares, stocks began to fall (see Figure 12-8). In four days, it was trading below its nine-day moving average, triggering an exit based on the strategy I described. I bought shares at $ 38.54 and a loss of 6.8% at $ 35.92. However, my sizing strategy (remember that I only bought 186 shares) limited the impact of this position on my account - I lost only 0.5% of my entire portfolio, which is a loss.

Step 8: Improve your swing trading skills

No swing dealer is perfect, and no trading system works 100% of the time. You will always suffer losses - they are inevitable. You should expect losses and work on your swing trading strategy. A good system was corrupted by an ambitious swing operator who was trying to achieve a simply unrealistic success rate.

But that does not mean you can not improve your system. One way to refine your system and become a better operator is to review your publications every month to detect trends in your winning or losing positions. But do not change your trading plan often or because of one or two lost trades. Change your plan only in response to a series of losses that you believe you can improve or in response to a significant - or potentially significant - loss (such as 5% or more of the total value of your account). For example, if your losses are large, you will probably need to adjust your risk management strategy rather than your inbound and outbound strategy.

EVALUATE YOUR PERFORMANCES

Recently, a trader asked me how I evaluated my performance as a trader and, for many, the answer may seem obvious. There is certainly more than one answer.

This is because there are many ways to evaluate our performance as traders, but let's look at two general categories for purposes of this article.

The most common way of evaluating performance is purely based on the results ... P & L, gain rate, maximum gain x maximum loss, maximum draft depth, etc. This is the quick conclusion that most people turn to, and these statistics are certainly important, especially for those who want to know the result.

The only problem with the data is that they tell only part of the story. Many traders know the result, but do not know where to find answers to improve it.

Crossing this bridge requires another strategy.

Another way to assess our performance as negotiators is to look closely at our trading process. This honestly and objectively can reveal very useful information to modify our business plan.

To achieve this, however, we must ask ourselves some difficult questions about the search for the truth, some of which may be:

• Do I have a specific plan for that trade and follow it?

• Am I taking plays which I understand that fit my trading schedule?

• Am I trading too large and, therefore, make bad decisions because I only answer to my profit and loss account?

• Am I getting ready for a trading day by doing my homework?

• Am I trading responsibly?

• Do I have reliable strategies that can make a profit over time?

I think the decisive factor between these two key assessments is the difference between the data and our state of mind. Sometimes we negotiate with the right attitude and good emotions, but our data needs to be corrected. Sometimes our data is a bit wrong, but what needs to be corrected is our attitude or mental approach (super trading, vengeance, neglect, fear, etc.). Knowing the symptoms will help us know which way to go.

I used to evaluate my data at the end of each month, but now that I am more experienced, my style of frequency and evaluation varies according to need. When things are going well, I do not appreciate much; I try to keep doing what works.

When I'm in a recession, I first see my routine to make sure everything is in order. Then I check my gain rate and determine if something is tarnishing it (like some chart models that do not work, for example). If I am still looking for a solution, I will check if my maximum gain x maximum loss during this period is out of sync or if my comparison between the average gain and the average loss size needs to change.

During this process, total honesty is required with myself; otherwise, I lose time. And as some things start to stand out, I'm going to impose restrictions or new rules to start stopping the bleeding, and I hope the ship is right.

So, the next time you want to start thinking about how your trading will go, be sure to look at different angles from your P & L account.

While this is the main thing, you are looking to improve on, considering some other areas of the trading process can provide a very useful insight into how you can increase your trading account.

CHAPTER SIX: THE BASICS OF DAY TRADING

Day traders often enter and exit trading positions, sometimes more than one period in a day. Day traders can even get in and out of a position of a minute to two.

Some players compare to see the graphics and jump quickly into positions, for the fast action and excitement of a video game. However, much more is at stake. Instead of just losing a game, a bad move can mean losing your entire wallet or more. Yes, day traders find themselves in negative positions because of money for the companies with which they are trading. We explain how this can happen later in this chapter.

For the moment, you should know that traders rarely have stock at night and that watching a computer screen for hours is an essential part of the day for this type of high-stress trading. Although none of us are or have ever been a day trader, in this chapter, we explain how this kind of high-risk trading works, we provide common strategies used by these types of traders, but we are also exploring the restrictions imposed on the United States. The Commission (SEC) puts operators on day traders and shows the high levels of risk they face.

GETTING STARTED WITH DAY TRADING

Earn money while sitting at home! Be your boss! Hit the market with your intelligence! Build real wealth! Tempting, is not it? Day trading can be the best way to make money on your own. It's also another way to lose a ton of money on your own. Do you possess that courage to face the market every morning?

Day trading is a crazy affair. Merchants work in front of their computer screens, reacting to blips, each representing real dollars. They take quick decisions because their ability to make money depends on the success of a lot of small profit negotiations. They close their positions on stocks, options, and futures that they own at the end of the day, which limits certain risks - nothing can happen overnight to disrupt an existing profit situation - but these limits risk can limit profits. After all, many things can happen in a year, increasing the likelihood that your business idea will work, but in a day? You must be patient and work fast. Some days, they offer nothing good to buy. Other days, every business seems to lose money.

The individual human negotiator faces a difficult adversary: high-frequency algorithms programmed and operated by brokerage firms and hedge funds that do not feel the emotion and can do business in less time than it takes to blink your eyes. If you are not prepared for this competition, you will be crushed.

It's All in a Day's Work: Defining Day Trading

The definition of day trading implies that day traders keep their titles for one day only. Their posioThey close their positions at the end of every day and then start the next day again. On the other hand, swing traders hold bonds for days and sometimes even months; investors sometimes stay for years. The short-term nature of the trading day reduces some risks because nothing can happen overnight to cause big losses. At the same time, many other types of investors go to bed thinking that their position is in excellent condition to wake up the next morning and discover that the company has announced huge profits or that its CEO is being charged with fraud.

But there is another side (there is always a disadvantage, is not it?): The choice of securities and positions of the day trader must work in the day or is over. Tomorrow does not exist for any particular post. Meanwhile, the swing trader or investor has the luxury of the time needed, as it sometimes takes a little time for your post to function as you should. In the long run, markets are efficient and effective, and prices reflect all the information about a bond. Unfortunately, it can take a few days for this effectiveness to materialize.

Day traders are speculators that work in zero-sum markets one day at a time. This makes the dynamics different from other types of financial activities in which you may be involved. When you adopt day trading, the rules that may have helped you choose good stocks or find great mutual funds over the years no longer apply. The trading day is a different game with different rules.

Speculate, do not hedge Professional traders fall into two categories: speculators and hedgers. Speculators seek to profit from price changes. The hedgers seek to protect themselves against a price change. They make sure that their buying and selling choices are safe and not a way to make a profit. They, therefore, choose positions that offset their exposure in another market.

As an example of coverage, consider a food processor and the farmer who creates or grows the ingredients that the company needs. The company may seek to guard against the risk of increased prices for key ingredients - such as corn, cooking oil or meat - by buying future contracts for these ingredients. So, if prices go up, the company's profits on the contracts will help finance the higher prices it will have to pay for these ingredients. If prices stay the same or fall, the company only loses the contract price, which can be fair compensation for the company. The producer of corn, soybean or livestock, on the other hand, will benefit if prices rise and suffer if they fall. To guard against a fall in prices, the farmer would sell futures on these products. Your futures position would earn money if the price went down, offsetting the decline of your products. And if prices went up, he would lose money on the contracts, but this loss would be offset by the gain in his crop.

Commodity markets were designed to help farmers manage risks and find buyers for their products. Stock and bond markets were created to encourage investors to finance businesses. Speculation appeared almost immediately in all these markets, but it was not his main objective.

Day traders are all speculators. They are looking to make money in the market as they see it now. They manage their risk by allocating their money carefully, using stop orders and limited orders (closing positions as soon as predetermined price levels are reached) and late evening. Day traders do not manage risk by offsetting their positions in the same way as a hedger. They use other techniques to limit losses, such as prudent money management and stop and limit orders.

The markets have hedgers and speculators. Knowing that different participants have different expectations of income and loss can help you navigate the flurry of activity on each trading day. And this is important because to make money on a zero-sum market; you only make money if another person loses.

DAY TRADING STRATEGIES

As discussed throughout this chapter, day traders trade shares in batches of 1,000 or more shares, exposing a large portion of their cash flow to each transaction. While the profit potential is high, you also risk losing all your money and maybe even money if you borrow money from your margin account.

Before considering day trading, you need to understand the risks you are taking and how to control them. Otherwise, money can come out of your account very quickly. Studies show that it usually takes six months to learn how to become a successful professional and that during this learning curve, you can lose money. The success rate of marketers ranges from 10% to 30% of those who try it. In other words, 70% to 90% of people who try day trading cannot and often do away with their indebted day trading career. We explain more about the risks in "The risks are high; The rewards can be huge," later in the chapter, but we must first review some of the basic strategies used by market operators.

Technical requirements

The number one list of things you need to become a marketer of the day is a good computer and an Internet setup. They are necessary for the commercial success of the day. Most traders possess two or more monitors with a PC built to handle a large number of data feeds at a time. Windows XP or Vista is the popular forms of day traders because most trading platforms are written for these environments and because they can handle multiple monitors.

Daily computer maintenance is essential for day traders. IT problems are the last thing you want to live in the middle of the trading day, especially when buying positions have been left open. You can lose more money if you wait until the computer restarts and the store disappears. Merchants advise you to clear cookies (files that websites send to your computer when you use them) from your Internet cache and defragment them every day (rearrange your files for the computer to work more efficiently). once a week

Another important step is to find a reliable Internet Service Provider (ISP) offering broadband Internet access. Many traders have more than one ISP online, so they have a backup in case the first one falls out.

Again, you do not want to lose even a few seconds when you are in the middle of a trading day, especially when you have open positions.

Trading Patterns

Day traders use models seen in a technical analysis similar to those discussed in the first part of this book. A common standard trader of the day is the price spread of stock at the opening of the market. They find that prices generally move in the same direction as the first price differential during the first few minutes when the market is open, and then the market tends to reverse and close the gap. Trading that does not close the gap during the first five to ten minutes may indicate a dominant trend for the day of that particular title. Some traders observe this action to find their goals for the day and the instructions they intend to play. Of course, there is no consensus on this. Others believe that early market movements give false signals and that using them to plan your trading day can be dangerous.

Traders observe many of the characteristics they encounter when looking for signs of escape and signs of turning. The main difference is that a day trader searches for intraday signals, while long-term traders format their charts for longer periods.

Scalping

Scalping means that you enter and exit a position for a very limited profit in a very short time, usually a few seconds or minutes. The scaler aims to generate profits from fractions of points maximum, instead of the different profit points sought by most traders. Day traders manage their business in a much shorter time. The money changers are only looking for 10 to 25 cents per share, hoping to make small gains as often as possible. When you use higher-priced stocks ($ 100 or more per share) or move faster, a stain can be considered a scalp.

For most stocks, scalping will not pay if you trade less than 1,000 shares. That's why a clear profit of 10 cents per 1,000 shares is only $ 100 before you pay a transaction or commission fee. There will be little profit after commissions and fees if you negotiate lots of less than 1,000 shares.

Traders trend

Not all marketers use the scalping technique. Some are trend traders. Instead of going in and out of a trade for a fraction of a point, they look for profits of at least one or two points and can stay in the same position for a few minutes or until one hour. Trend traders are doing less business than money changers, but they are looking for higher profits per company and can trade blocks of less than a thousand shares because they can make a good profit as trend traders with a volume greatly reduced stock. Traders looking for more than one point sometimes earn a stock for several hours, unless the stock is expensive or their price is changing rapidly.

The risks are high; Rewards can also be high

By learning about the trading patterns and the high volume of stock trading, you have probably already discovered for yourself that the risks are high. In a matter of minutes, getting in and out of stocks in blocks of thousands of shares can be tedious when a stock moves quickly in a direction you did not anticipate.

The US Senate investigated the risks of day trading after a shootout in a commercial center in Atlanta, Georgia, killing nine people in July 1999. Sniper Mark Barton was a chemist before getting involved in day trading and lose $ 105,000 in just one month. He killed himself after the shot.

Senate investigators found that the revenues of the 15 largest day trading companies in 1999 were $ 541.5 million, 276% higher than their 1997 revenues. Profits increased by more than $66 million and by 2000 the 15 companies have opened 12,000 new accounts. The researchers also found that the 4,000 to 5,000 most active operators take huge amounts of money and lose it. Also, in the year 2000, traders paid an average of $ 16 per transaction and averaged 29 transactions per day. Using these statistics, the researchers concluded that a trader needed to earn more than $ 111,000 a year in stock market earnings to balance that level of costs.

A second study, published in May 2004 by university professors who analyzed daily traders on the Taiwan Stock Exchange, found that 82% of traders were losing money. Some can make money almost every day, but end up losing money after calculating running costs.

Liquidity

To be termed liquid, a trader must have the ability to turn the stock into cash quickly. Although you may find that a day trader has to trade a large number of stocks to make a profit, he must also have significant cash and securities in his account to continue his trading activities.

Avoiding common mistakes

If the risks and costs do not scare you off the trading day, you have to familiarize yourself with some common mistakes leading to the failure of many traders of the day. Some traders talk about their most common mistakes, especially those that cost a lot of money when building their business. Here are some of the most serious mistakes made by new traders:

✓ **Break Stop Loss rules:** When a stock starts to fall, newer, not yet disciplined, traders tend to panic when their choices start losing money, so they decide to keep the stock instead of leaving it when their first stop is reached. However, traders will use this strategy because they do not stop their losses as expected. You must ensure to set your exit prices based on your technical profit and loss analysis when you purchase the stock for the first time. Follow these rules mechanically when the target price is reached and do not let your emotions get in the way.

✓ **Chasing Trends:** New traders who do not know how to read the standards are usually waiting to see if they are right before entering a position. This hesitation causes them to lose entry points and, if they are right, they may end up forcing them to buy at a higher stock price than they expected when an upward trend is expected or selling at a reduced price than they intended when a downward trend is expected. In the absence of desired entry prices, traders eventually follow trends and find that their original entry points and exit points are no longer valid, as many others have already taken action and stocks are no longer available at scheduled prices. Experienced traders are simply coming out of this trade instead of getting involved in trading platforms that are not technical analysis and are continuing a trend.

✓ **Always wait for the right trade:** a new day trader must show the patience necessary to hope that the right contract matches what the technical analysis indicates. Experienced traders know how to wait for the right moment rather than forcing a deal, picking the wrong price, and overexploiting the account.

✓ **Always set rules before the start of the trading day:** to avoid getting lost in the emotions of a major gain or loss, you must determine your entry and exit points before the start of trading and never divert them after the start of the day. Experienced traders know that you are focusing on your business or thinking about your rules. You do not have time to do both, and trying to do this can be a recipe for disaster. It is essential to remain objective and respect your rules to maintain the necessary control of a day trader.

✓ **Forget that fundamentals matter little:** novice traders understand that the company they buy the stock is a good company, and when their shares lose ground, they are forced to step back. Experienced traders know that the appearance of fundamentals does not matter and that when the market sells, even the price of a good stock falls. Day traders must follow market signals and not worry about the quality or disadvantages of the fundamentals of the company they market.

✓ **Average:** although investors may fall, which means they buy a stock and, if the price goes down, they buy even more shares, thinking it's a good stock that will recover, this technique does not work for day traders, and most experienced traders of all varieties will tell you that using it is a fatal mistake. Day traders think rather that you have to set a stop price and an exit price (called stop) for a lost stock and possibly return to it at a lower price. In doing so, you have the time to objectively examine what is happening in the stock and determine if it is worth it. You are also likely to stop spending less than the average and not run the risk of having a margin problem. Doing a downward average can incur a lot of money that could otherwise be used for more profitable trading with a different stock. The worst feeling, even for a seasoned professional, is when a stock falls well below the stopping position because it's hard to decide if the loss is important. In most cases, if you do not know the next step, experienced traders advise you to leave this position before the situation gets worse or gets out of hand.

✓ **Not knowing when to make a profit:** Newcomers sometimes make the mistake of making a profit early or not making a profit. Both can lead to unnecessary losses. Most of the time, indecision occurs when traders are afraid of losing profits if they stay too long or leave too early. As with losses, exit points must be determined before entering a position, and rules must be followed. Remember that as a day trader, you need to focus on your trading or your rules. Day traders who are used to entering and exiting positions in seconds or minutes do not have time to do both.

✓ **Move away from the computer with open positions:** experienced traders never leave their computer when they still have an open position. Although we briefly examine the maintenance of open positions at night in the introduction to this chapter, this rule is even more rigid. While experienced day traders react to price changes in seconds or minutes, they do not want to stay away from the screen as long as a position is still open.

CHAPTER SEVEN: MAXIMIZING POTENTIAL RETURN WITH SHORT SELLING AND LEVERAGE

In a sense, the trading day is not risky. Day traders close their positions overnight to minimize the risk of problems when traders pay no attention. Every business is based on discovering a small price change on the market for a short time. It is, therefore, not likely that anything will change dramatically. But here's the thing: trading in this way leads to small returns. Full-time trading is difficult to justify if you do not make a lot of money doing it, regardless of your level of risk.

And a few days, there is not much good business to do. You may be looking for titles to climb, but this is not the case. Zero transactions lead to zero risk - and zero return. For this reason, savvy traders think of other ways to earn money in their business, even when it involves more risk. This risk is what generates the desired return by many marketers.

THE SWITCH-UP OF SHORT SELLING

Traditionally, traders and investors want to purchase low and sell high. They buy a position in a bond and then expect the price to rise. This strategy is not a bad strategy to make money, especially because if the country's economy continues to grow a little, companies will grow and their actions too.

But even in a good economy, some bonds fall. The company can be poorly managed; it can sell an obsolete product or have only a sequence of bad days. Incidentally, the price may have risen a bit too much, and investors are finding their reason again. In these situations, you can not make money buying cheap and selling a lot. Instead, you need a way to reverse the situation.

The solution? Short Sale In Brief - hah! Selling short means that you are borrowing a bond and selling it in the hope of repaying the purchase loan by buying less expensive shares.

In business language, when you have something, you are considered long. When you sell, especially if you do not already have it, you are considered to be short. You do not have to be long before you become short.

Selling Short

Most brokerages make selling short easy. You place an order to sell the shorts, and the broker asks you if you are selling shares of your property or short sales. After making the request, the brokerage borrows shares that you can sell. He lends the shares to his account and executes the sales order.

You can not sell short unless the broker can lend the shares. Sometimes, many people sell shares in the open without a stock being borrowed. In this case, you must find another action or strategy.

When you sell the shares, you wait until the price of security drops, and then you purchase the shares in the market at a good price. You then return the purchased shares to the broker to repay the loan, and you keep the difference between the point of sale and the place of purchase - minus interest, of course.

The stock exchanges help companies to raise money, therefore, have rules to maintain a bullish bias on the stock market. These rules may not favor the short seller. The main rule is a so-called increase rule, which means that you can only sell a stock short when the last transaction was an increase. You can not reduce a declining stock.

The fees and interest that the broker charges to the operators who borrow shares accrue to the broker, not to the person who owns the shares. The owner of the stock will probably never know that his stock has been borrowed.

Choose shorts

Investors - people who do extensive research and expect to hold office for months to years - are looking for companies that have inflated expectations and may be fraudulent. Investors who work in the short-term market spend hours doing careful accounting research and looking for companies whose price might fall sometimes.

Day traders do not care about accounting. They do not have time to wait for a short event to happen. Instead, they are looking for stocks whose prices are falling for more mundane reasons, such as more sellers than buyers within the next fifteen minutes. Most day traders who sell short reverse their long-term strategy. For example, some traders like to buy stocks that have fallen three days in a row, imagining that they will go up on the fourth day. They will also have short-term stocks that have risen three days in a row, imagining they will fall on the fourth day. You do not need a CPA to do it!

Trading strategies have been discussed in details in earlier chapters if you are looking for ideas.

To lose your shorts?

Listed shares carry certain risks because a short sale is a bet on things that go wrong. Because theoretically, the stock can go up without limits, there is no limit to the amount of money that a short seller may lose. Two traps, in particular, can bring a seller to the open. The first is a short press due to the good news; the second is a concerted effort to hurt the small traders.

Squeeze my shorts

With a short squeeze, a company that has been popular with many short sellers has good news that raises the stock price. Or maybe other buyers increase the price to force the sale of shorts, which is a common form of market manipulation. When the price increases, short sellers lose money, and some may even have margin problems. And it can be proved that the primary reason for the short position is wrong.

Those with little money are starting to buy stocks to reduce their losses, but the growing demand is causing a further rise in stock prices, resulting in even greater losses for people who are still low. Oh!

Recall the stock

All is not soft and light in the world of short sales. Many market players are wary of people doing all the research carefully, in part because they are often right. The company's executives are generally optimistic and do not like to hear bad news. They blame sellers for all that is wrong with the stock price. Meanwhile, we know that some short sellers get impatient and start spreading unpleasant rumors if selling them does not generate money.

Many companies, brokers, and investors hate short sellers and try tactics to reduce them. Sometimes they send good news or spread good rumors to create a squeeze. At other times, they collectively ask stockholders to ask their brokerage firms not to lend their shares, which means that those who have shortened their stock must buy back and return shares, even if that does not make any sense.

Borrowing in Your Trading Business

Leverage is only a part of the borrowings associated with your day trading business. Like any business owner, you sometimes need more money than your business generates. At other times, you see opportunities for expansion that require more money than you have on hand. In this section, I discuss why and how day traders can borrow money in addition to leveraged trading.

Borrow a marginal cash flow

If day trading is your job, you are under constant pressure: how to cover the costs of living while keeping enough money on the market to negotiate? A better way to do this is to have another source of income - savings, spouse, or work that does not overlap with market hours. Other day traders draw money from your trading account.

If the market does not cooperate, your account may not have enough resources to allow the withdrawal of funds and, at the same time, maintain sufficient capital to negotiate. One option is to obtain a margin loan from a brokerage firm.

With a margin loan, the company allows you to make a loan against the money in your account (or bonds that you hold, not transactions). You can spend the cash as you see fit, but you have to repay it. Nevertheless, a margin loan is a good option because the benefits of daily transactions tend to be erratic.

Borrowing for trading capital

One day, traders use double leverage: they borrow money to set up their trading accounts and then lend money to their trading strategies. If the market cooperates, this type of loan can be a great way to make money, but if the market does not cooperate, you can end up with a lot of money that you do not have.

If you want to take the risk, however, you have resources to turn into other people who are not your loved ones: you can borrow against your house, use your credit cards or find a company that gives you money to work.

Borrowing against your house

Yes, you can use a mortgage or line of credit to get the money you need for day trading. In general, this option has low-interest rates because your home is your guarantee. In most cases, however, interest is not tax deductible (ask your accountant, but generally you can only deduct the interest used to buy or improve your home). Nevertheless, borrowing against your home can be a relatively inexpensive way to get the value stored in your home for commercial use.

The risk? If you can not repay the loan, you risk losing your home. If you decide to follow this strategy, do not borrow your car either, because you will need a place to live when the bank is closed.

Putting it on the card

The business world is filled with people who have started using credit cards. And you can do that. If you have good credit, credit card companies will be happy to lend you.

Of course, credit card companies charge a high interest rate, which even the savviest traders will find difficult to cover with their returns.

If the only way to raise capital for the trading day is to use your credit card, remember to wait a few years and save your money before making the jump. Since day trading can be irregular, you can use your credit cards to cover your expenses for a few months. You may want to save your credit for this instead of spending it directly on your trading day.

Accept risk capital from a brokerage firm

Some companies active in the trade are willing to attract new traders. You may need to complete a training period or pay a fee to rent an office in your office or use your software remotely. The company observes its business practices, including earnings and risk management. If administrators like what they see, they can offer you money to manage with your capital. You will receive some part of the profits from the funds you have negotiated to obtain them.

Free riding costs

Some traders understand that they do not need margin accounts if they buy a cash account and sell it before paying it. It's called free riding, and the SEC does not look like that. Brokerage firms are forced to freeze a client's account for 90 days when they identify free to use. The customer can then exchange only if he pays for each transaction as it is done, instead of receiving the three days normally outsourced.

If you are trading on a cash account, you can avoid a freeze by paying for the purchased securities within a maximum of three days, without relying on money from the sale of these securities to cover the payment. The alternative is to exchange a margin account.

RISK AND REWARD ASSESSMENT FROM SHORT SELLING AND LEVERAGE

Leverage introduces risk for your trading day, which can earn you a lot more. Most day, traders use leverage, at least part of the time, for their trading activities to be cold. The challenge is to use the lever responsibly. Here, I cover the two most important problems: losing your money and losing your courage. Understanding these risks can help you determine what leverage you should take and how often you can accept it.

Losing your money

Losing money is an obvious danger. Leverage increases your returns but also increases your risk. All loans must be paid independently. If you sell or purchase a futures contract or options, you are legally required to perform even if you have lost money. It can be very difficult.

The trading day is risky, largely because of the leverage used. If you do not feel comfortable with this, you can use little or no leverage, especially when you start trading in day trading or when you start working on a new trading strategy.

Losing your nerves

The base risk and the return of the underlying strategy are not affected by the leverage. If you expect your system to work about 60% of the time, it should happen, regardless of the amount of money involved or the source of the money. However, trading with borrowed money probably makes a difference for you on a subconscious level.

Negotiation is a lot more nerves. If you hesitate to negotiate, reduce a loss, or follow your strategy, you will have problems. Suppose you are trading futures and you decide to accept three declines before you sell, and you will need five adjustments before you sell. This strategy means that you are ready to accept a loss, reduce it if you lose control of your situation, and accept the gains when you get them. This allows you to limit your losses while imposing some discipline on your earnings. Now, suppose you have a lot of weight. Suddenly, these slowdowns become too real for you - it's money you do not have. The next thing you know, you only accept two stops before closing. But this prevents you from winning winners. So, you decide to walk with your winners, and suddenly, you do not take advantage quickly enough, and your positions move against you. Your fear of loss makes you sloppy. This is why many marketers find it preferable to ask for less money and join the system than to lend as much as they can and to let that knowledge disturb their judgment.

Lenders can also lose their nerves. Your broker may close your account due to losses, although waiting a little longer can turn a lost position into profit. Do you remember Bear Stearns, the big old brokerage firm that closed in March 2008? Or Lehman Brothers, the big brokerage firm that closed in September 2008? Both were closed because they suffered heavy losses and their creditors gave them no money.

CONCLUSION - STRATEGIES OF 2020 THAT WORKS

Swing Trading is not a strategy but a style. The defined period defines this style and contains many strategies that we can use to promote commerce. Swing trading is a style that operates in the short and medium term. You are among the very short trading times of the day and the longest terms of position trading.

It's not so short that it takes all your time watching the market, but it's short enough to offer many business opportunities. These strategies are not unique to swing trading and, as is the case with most technical resistance, strategies, and support are the key concepts that underlie them.

These concepts offer you two options within your swing trading strategy, including following the trend or the trading counter for the trend. Antitrust strategies tend to be profitable when levels of support and resistance remain. Trend monitoring strategies look for times when levels of support and resistance collapse.

For all types, it is useful to be able to recognize the price action visually. A quick word on price action:

Markets do not tend to move in a straight line. Even when they finally tend to go up and down gradually. We recognize an uptrend for the market, setting highs and lows, and identifying lower lows. Several swing trading strategies include trying to catch and follow a short trend.

In the second strategy, we do not define a limit. Why do not we use a limit? Because we want to manage our profits as long as possible. We do not know how long the trend can persist or how high the market can go. As a result, we will not try to predict by setting a price target, but we know that prices do not increase directly.

This means that you have to let the market move in a negative way to some extent to define the trend properly. It also means that when the trend breaks, you will have returned some of your unrealized profits before closing. Instead of using a limit, we will stop at least in the last 20 periods.

We have never changed this stop: if a minimum of 20 hours is greater than our previous stop, we will increase our stop to a minimum of 20 hours. In general, this means that our judgment is following the trend. The graph below shows that this strategy would upset us if the price fell abruptly at 3 pm on July 15th.

Do you want to know the good news?

In the long run: with good risk management, profits must outweigh losses when the trend collapses.

Our 3rd swing trading strategy is more of contending trade and therefore, the opposite of the first two. We use the same principles to try to detect construction trends in the short term: we are now trying to utilize the advantage of the frequency with which these tendencies tend to fall apart.

Remember this, as previously stated:

• Higher values suggest a bullish trend

• Small declines suggest a downward trend

We have also seen how the first part of a trend can be followed by a withdrawal period before the trend resumes. A counter-trend trader would try to take the shock in this period of turnaround. To do this, we would try to recognize the uptrend pattern. So, when a new summit was followed by a series of failures to break new heights, we anticipated such a reversal.

In the case of counter-trend, it is very important to maintain a strict discipline if the price fluctuates against you. You must be willing to admit that you are wrong and draw a line in the trade if the market resumes its trend against you. All the strategies we have discussed so far are very simple. They can recognize and understand price action.

What can marketers do to improve their strategies? However, there are several things you can try. The first is to try to combine the trade with the long-term trend. Although in the examples above, we looked at an hourly chart, it may also be useful to look at a longer-term chart - to get an idea of the long-term trend. Try to negotiate only when your direction is what you consider a long-term trend.

Another method to improve your strategy is to make use of a secondary technical indicator to confirm your reasoning. For example, if you plan to sell against the grain and you plan to sell, check the Relative Strength Index (RSI) and see if it indicates that the market is overbought.

A moving average (MA) is another indicator that you could use to help you. Mastery softens prices to give a clearer view of the trend. And since an MA incorporates older price data, it is easy to compare current prices with lower prices.

Swing trading is a style best suited to volatile markets and offers frequent trading opportunities. Although you need a lot of time to monitor the market with swing trading, the requirements are not as cumbersome as short-term trading styles. Again, swing trading is not ideal for all traders - so it's best to start trading safely in a demo account.

We also examined some entry and exit strategies for swing trading. But it is essential to note that a complete trading system will also incorporate good money management and will be able to identify the right markets.

Some other good practices are:

• avoid trading against the general trend of the market

• Use a secondary indicator to confirm the signal of your main indicator.

• Have a clear idea of your exit limit and keep it below the profit you are targeting.

If you can follow all the strategies described in this book, you will surely become a successful professional trader soon.